RELIGION IN THE MODERN WORLD

LORD NORTHBOURNE

RELIGION IN THE MODERN WORLD

Edited by

Christopher James
5th Lord Northbourne

INCLUDING
CORRESPONDENCE WITH
THOMAS MERTON

SOPHIA PERENNIS

GHENT NY

Second, revised and expanded edition
Sophia Perennis, Ghent NY
First edition 1963, J.M. Dent & Sons, LTD London
© Christopher James Northbourne 2001
Letters 'To Lord Northbourne' Easter 1965,
February 23, 1966, August 30, 1966, and June 4, 1967
from *Witness to Freedom* by Thomas Merton,
edited by William H. Shannon. Copyright © 1994
by the Merton Legacy Trust. Reprinted by permission
of Farrar, Straus and Giroux, LLC.

General editor: James R. Wetmore

For information, address:
Sophia Perennis, 343 Rte 21C
Ghent NY 12075

By the same author

Look to the Land
Looking Back on Progress

Library of Congress Cataloging-in-Publication Data

Northbourne, Lord, 1896–1982
Religion in the modern world / Lord Northbourne. — 2nd, rev. ed.
Edited by Christopher James, 5th Lord Northbourne.

p. cm.
Includes index.
ISBN 0 900588 57 8 (pbk: alk. paper)
1. Christianity—Essence, genius, nature. 2. Religion. I. Title.
BT60.N6 2001
200—dc21   2001000867

CONTENTS

INTRODUCTION

THIS short treatise contains nothing which is in substance new. It is a restatement of ideas which for the greater part of human history have been considered axiomatic. It is also an assessment of their relevance to modern conditions.

The point of view adopted here is one that risks being regarded as reactionary. It is not reactionary precisely and only insofar as it is in conformity with truth. With the same proviso it is also not progressive, for truth is neither progressive nor reactionary but wholly independent of human attitudes. Truth does not change because it is expressed in a different way, nor because opinions change, nor because it may not fit in with individual or collective likes and dislikes. It remains what it is and was and always will be, whether man remembers it or not.

This is the truth of which Meister Eckhart spoke when he said, in effect, that if he had to choose between God and truth, he would choose truth and abandon God; but that question does not arise, because God is Truth. He was speaking of Absolute Truth, which transcends and comprehends its own reflection in the relative. It is the reflection we are usually thinking of when we speak about truth. Only Absolute Truth is immutable; only relative truth can be expressed in words. Relative truth derives its 'trueness' from the fact that it is a reflection, however dim, of Absolute Truth.

Absolute Truth itself is inexpressible because it comprehends not only all that exists but also all possibility. Since Absolute Truth is immutable, its reflected image can never be something other than it; it can only be more or less dim or distorted. It can also, like a terrestrial reflection, be inverted.

Everything that exists is but a reflection of Absolute Truth, but some things reflect it more clearly, more directly and in a manner more adapted to our understanding than others. Some, being inverted reflections, appear to deny it, although all they are really doing is to affirm its comprehensiveness, which includes the possibility of its own negation.

If religion, in itself and in principle, is in the category of direct reflections of absolute Truth, and if it is first in that category both as to its directness and as to its adaptation to human comprehension, then it is greater than man and exists in its own right independently of what man makes of it, and man is judged by it.

If on the other hand, as some would assert, religion is a by-product of human nature and nothing more, then it exists only by and through man. It is less than him, so he can judge it.

There is no more vital distinction than that between what judges us as men, and what we as men are entitled to judge. It seems today to be all too frequently taken for granted that there is nothing that we are not entitled to judge. Indeed in these days there is nothing that is not called in question—even religion. The word religion itself is often used so loosely as to include things that are, as nearly as possible, its contraries. There is nothing that is not considered a matter of opinion, and therefore at the mercy of mental and verbal juggling. There appears to be no stable and authoritative source of truth. Religion is neglected and despised and its enemies flourish. One of their main objectives is to create confusion, not only as to what religion is and is not, but also as to the disguises they themselves assume.

The purpose of this treatise is to do something to lessen the confusion that prevails on these two points.

1

RELIGION
& TRADITION

THE word 'religion' is often used today simply to mean whatever an individual or a group regards as being true, or that whereby conduct is regulated. Even Communism is sometimes loosely called a religion, regardless of its origin and its tendencies, and regardless of the fact that it is no more than a construction of the human mind. Such things as Communism may be substitutes for religion, but to call them religions is an abuse of the word which can give rise to a very pernicious kind of confusion.

In its original and only valid sense the word 'religion' applies only to something which is, above all, not a construction of the human mind, but is, on the contrary, of divine origin, so that it can be said to be supernatural, revealed or mysterious. Its purpose is to provide an effective link between the world and God. The word 'Religion' is always used hereafter in this strict sense, and to emphasize this it is spelt with a capital R.

All that follows is applicable to the Christian Religion. In the main it is also applicable to what are sometimes called the great Religions of the world. It is assumed here that each has its validity for a particular group of peoples, despite outward differences and even apparent contradictions. What matters for each person is adherence to one Religion, normally that of the country of one's birth, rather than attempts to reconcile it with others, or purely academic excursions into the field of comparative religion.

The completeness and uniqueness of a Religion implies that from the point of view of its followers it is preferable to any other. It really is so for them, but not necessarily for other people. There may often be good reason for defending it against other Religions in order to preserve its purity and the coherence of its symbolism. That does not alter the fact that all 'orthodox' Religions—that is to say those that are linked by an unbroken chain of tradition to an authentic Revelation—are paths that lead to the same summit. If that were not so, God would have denied the possibility of salvation to a vast majority of the earth's inhabitants, past and present. It is surprising how cheerfully many of the followers of a Religion based on love and charity accept this conclusion.

Paths that lead to a summit are widely separated near the base of the mountain, but they get nearer together as they rise. The wise climber takes the path on which he finds himself and does not worry too much about people on other paths. He can see his path but cannot see theirs properly. He will waste an enormous amount of his own time if he keeps on trying to find another and better path. He will waste other people's time if he tries to persuade them to abandon theirs, however sure he is that his is the best.

Religion is founded on the belief—or rather on the certainty— that God has shown His love, as well as His justice and His wisdom, to the world in the first place and most directly in His Revelation of Himself through the founder (or founders) of the Religion in question. This implies that the founder did not invent that Religion, his part being entirely receptive, insofar as a distinction can be made between his divine and human nature.

Revelation is therefore by definition something greater than anything purely human, including reason. Its validity is beyond rational or observational proof or disproof; nevertheless it would not be what it is if it did not contain internally the evidence of its own truth. That evidence will be acceptable or discernible or self-evident to the eye of faith or of wisdom, although it may not be accessible to analytical investigation.

Revelation enters into the definition of Religion because it is the foundation of everything in the world that has hitherto been called Religion—and not least of the Christian Religion. Revealed Religion does not deny the possibility of individual inspiration—far from it; but it offers itself as the one universal and accessible means of grace available to all both collectively and individually, and as a framework within which individual inspiration can thrive unimpeded and can exercise its influence freely.

In His infinite Mercy, God has given us both freedom and a means of grace. Can we expect to be able to claim the one and refuse the other with impunity? Religion therefore implies not only an abstract belief in God, but also a concrete belief in His Revelation of Himself, His 'descent into form'. The imitation of that form then becomes the concrete or practical aspect of Religion, the means whereby it is made real and effective in the world rather than being merely notional or theoretical.

From this point of view, man is much more than a mere thinking animal. He is privileged above all other creatures in being given dominion over them as well as by the gifts of reason and of free will. Those privileges are accorded to him in his capacity as responsible guardian of revealed Religion, and for no other reason.

If, like all other creatures, man could not help following the commandments of God, as the plant cannot help turning towards the sun, then his situation would be neutral with respect to good and evil as theirs is. There would then be open to him no possibility better than this world—no heaven; and correlatively no possibility worse than this world—no hell.

The whole duty of man, and his whole advantage, reside in the preservation intact of the chain of tradition that connects him with Revelation. This applies with particular force in these days to the more specifically religious aspect of tradition.[1]

The word 'Tradition' will hereafter be spelt with a capital T because it suffers from the same kind of vague usage as the word 'Religion'. It is often used as if it were equivalent to 'custom' or 'style'. Properly speaking, Tradition comprises all the distinctive characteristics that are derived from the past, and make a civilization what it is, including those that can be more specifically described as religious. Religion could be said to be the way whereby man serves God most directly. The other aspects of Tradition comprise all the less

---

1. There are others that have been largely forgotten, or that survive unnoticed.

direct, but scarcely less essential ways, such as service to a hierarchical superior, obedience to the appropriate laws, defending Tradition against assaults from without, and so on.

The notion of Tradition is no mere arbitrary or invented one. Its foundations lie at the very root of our being. It can be accounted for in a way that is exceedingly simple and impregnably logical—for anyone who understands it. The Beginning and the End are the same;[2] therefore to be effectively linked to the Beginning is already to have found the End.

✠

If these notions of Revelation and Tradition are accepted, it becomes evident that a Revelation must be accepted as a whole and not in part. The doctrinal, ritual and ethical prescriptions of Religion are inseparable. A belief in God which rejects any of them is not Religion; indeed it is precisely one of those compromises by which people try to salve their consciences without too much trouble. Such a belief in God may perhaps be better than nothing, but it is something purely individual, whereas Religion is supra-individual. This is a very vital point.

The three elements mentioned—*doctrinal*, *ritual*, and *ethical*—can be discerned in every Religion. There is a correspondence between them and the three main divisions of the human faculties—intellectual, active and volitive—so that Religion neglects nothing human. These three elements will now be considered in order.

Doctrine is fundamental. It is the intellectual element concerned with the comprehension and formulation of truth and the combating of falsehood. As such it is necessarily the province of a relatively small intellectual elect which stands at the head of a hierarchy through which the truth is interpreted to the multitude in a form which they can accept.

2. 'I am Alpha and Omega,' Rev. 1:8.

However simple the primary formulation of a truth may appear to be (for example, 'God is Love'), its interpretation in terms of common experience is anything but simple. Insofar as the more elevated aspects of truth are concerned it must inevitably be dogmatic. Dogma and dogmatism are almost terms of abuse in these days. It is true enough that dogmatism applied to human affairs which are matters of opinion or of taste cannot be justified, but the case is very different when Religion is concerned. Dogma is a necessary feature of a Religion which is intended for everyone, since a large majority are not capable of grasping the more profound doctrinal truths in any other form. A doctrine fully comprehensible to the average intelligence would not be very profound. It would be intellectually insignificant and so would have no defense against perversion.

For example, every Religion either insists on the reality of heaven and hell, or expresses the same fundamental truth in a different way. This insistence is dogmatic, in the sense that heaven and hell represent something that is by definition beyond the limits of life on earth. They cannot be proved or disproved by means that appertain to that life on earth alone. Nevertheless if there is something greater than man there must also be a life greater than human life. That life is not subject to the same limitations as human life and so not imaginable or ascertainable by the individual as such. Some would accept this insofar as it relates to heaven, but not to hell. This is pure sentimentalism. Either man is not free to choose, a mere machine without responsibility, or he is free to choose and must take the consequences of his choice. No question of arbitrary reward or punishment is involved; it is merely a question of cause and effect.[3]

Ritual is the second essential element in Religion. It is derived directly from the original Revelation, which it recapitulates in a certain sense. This is particularly evident in the case of the Eucharist.

3. The perspective of reward and punishment is nevertheless legitimate and useful, otherwise it would not be characteristic of several Religions. Essentially it is simply an application of the law of compensation. As in so many other cases, a symbolical presentation in terms of familiar human situations brings the truth much nearer for most people than could any presentation in less familiar terms. This generation, with its literalism, has lost the habit of thinking in symbols: hence,

God must be worshipped not only in thought and word but also in deed. No act proceeding from the human will alone could adequately meet this need; God has therefore told us what we must do. However simple a ritual based on revelation may appear to be, we can be sure that its significance is inexhaustible and that its mysterious power extends beyond the confines of this world. It is effective simply by virtue of what it is and independently of the degree to which we may think we understand it. All this of course applies only to ritual that can be said to be strictly 'orthodox', in the sense that it is an integral part of a revealed Religion. Without ritual there is no Religion.

Closely associated with the specific acts appertaining to an orthodox ritual, and not independent of it, is the reading or recitation of the Sacred Scriptures and the recitation of a revealed or canonical form of prayer (e.g., The Lord's Prayer). Such reading and recitation are not effective outside the framework of the Religion to which they belong. Within that framework they are indispensable. This is particularly true in these days when the psychic environment, instead of being traditional and thereby providing an ever-present corrective to error, is so actively hostile and subversive. The effectiveness of this reading and recitation is not conditional on a purely mental comprehension. In the absence of its corrective influence the soul has no point of reference, no anchorage, no refuge, nothing to which it can—and must—return again and again in its inevitable wanderings. There can be no substitute for these indispensable graces.

There is one other grace, closely related to those last mentioned, whose benefit is strictly contingent on a traditional attachment. It takes many different forms in different Traditions: a divine Name or Names, a formula or a visible symbol. It is as it were incorporated in the gift of the original Revelation. It is an essential element in the

---

among other things, its difficulty in understanding the Holy Scriptures. Symbolism, however, is not only every bit as precise as literalism, but also much less limitative. Literalism narrows the truth, symbolism broadens and enlivens it without in any way departing from it. A symbol in this sense is a reflection on the terrestrial plane of a truth subsisting on a higher plane. The symbol, whether it be dogmatic in form or not, is therefore the necessary vehicle of doctrine.

formulae or prayers used in the methods of spiritual training associated with many Religions. No gift of God is more precious than this.

The third element is the ethical or moral. Without virtue the soul cannot become fit to be a receptacle of grace. That is what virtue is for; it is by no means mere social convenience.

The two other elements of Religion are concerned with man's relation to God, and therefore with the first ('and great') of the two New Testament commandments. Virtue is concerned with man's relation to his 'neighbor', that is, with everything that is not himself, but most immediately with his human neighbor. The neighbor exists by the will of God, so that to serve him is to serve God, and to offend him is to offend God. That is why the second commandment is 'like unto' the first; it also explains why in giving offence the soul harms itself more than its victim.

As to what constitutes offence, the best guidance is that afforded by the code of conduct or legislation that forms part of every Tradition. This may not be the same everywhere because of differences in conditions. Virtue is indispensable, but it is not an end in itself. Its efficacy reaches beyond the confines of the social field in which its operation is usually considered, and indeed beyond the confines of this world.

The first of the two commandments is greater than the second, but neither can be dispensed with. They are not essentially different, but only accidentally so. A single celestial truth is manifested terrestrially in two different modes.

Superimposed on the threefold division outlined above there is another division, much less easily defined. Every Religion has an exoteric, dogmatic and moral aspect, and an esoteric, metaphysical and mystical aspect. The two may not be rigidly separated, and the latter may be little more than an intensification of the former. Sometimes they are separated, and may have distinct names: for instance in the Far East they are called respectively Confucianism and Taoism; in Judaism the esoteric aspect is called the Kabbala, and in Islam, Sufism, or Tasawuuf. In Christianity and Buddhism there is no real separation, though in practice the esoteric aspect is the province of specialized organizations, often of a monastic type.

Esoterism is necessarily the province, or the calling, of a specially qualified and trained minority. It takes so many forms that no attempt at description could be satisfactory. Esoterism is the 'heart' of Religion, and exoterism the 'body'. Esoterism, broadly speaking, is the repository and guardian of the mystery or secret which is the mainspring of Religion. By its derivation (from the Greek 'to keep the mouth shut') the word 'mystery' does not mean something that is unknown, but something that cannot be absolutely or adequately expressed in words, but which is not for that reason unknowable. That is always its meaning when it is used in connection with Religion. The Greek mysteries were the esoteric aspect of their Religion and mythology.

The resemblance between the words 'secret' and 'sacred' is no accident.[4] The modern hatred and suspicion of the secret, of everything that is not laid open to public inspection, is also a hatred of the sacred, and of the 'mysterious' in the true sense of the word. The mystery is secret because it is inexpressible, and it is inexpressible because it concerns the Infinite, about which nothing exhaustive can be said, because speech and thought are always in some way limitative.

As we have seen, it is the specific function of humanity, occupying as it does a central position in the world, to keep that world in touch with the Infinite. Within humanity it is the specific function of those who follow an esoteric path to apprehend the mystery of the Infinite as directly as possible. The apprehension of those who follow an exoteric way is less direct, but none the less real. Its foundation is belief rather than vision, but there may not always in fact be a rigid line of demarcation.

From all this it is easy to see that the choice between adherence to Religion and its neglect or rejection has something absolute about it. If Religion is true, then there is nothing else that really counts, and the only practical thing to do is to follow it as best one can. If it

---

4. Chap. 8, p 69.

is untrue, then the only thing to do is to 'eat, drink and be merry, for tomorrow we die'. There can be no compromise. Religion cannot be an optional extra.

The choice between the acceptance or rejection of a particular form of Religion does not always seem to be as simple as the above would imply. The Religion we choose must be orthodox in the sense that in the first place it is derived from an authentic Revelation, and in the second place that it is connected to its origin by an unbroken chain of Tradition. This means that it must be neither heretical nor schismatic. The criterion of orthodoxy is conformity to a traditional law and symbolism, and to an intrinsic truth. However, the boundary between legitimate adaptation and deviation may sometimes be extremely difficult to define.

The preceding pages have been devoted to the presentation of certain positive criteria. Those that follow deal with certain modern tendencies in relation to the decay of Religion—or more accurately of religious faith, for Religion as such remains what it always was. They may help to indicate for some a basis for the exercise of a corresponding negative discrimination.

2

MODERNISM:
THE PROFANE
POINT OF VIEW

THE contemporary decay of Religion is not an isolated phenomenon. It is not confined to a restricted domain distinct from the secular domain. It is part of a fundamental change of point of view in relation to the nature of man and of the universe.

Whenever a people has lived in and by Religion—or more broadly Tradition—there may have been abuses and superstitions, incomprehension, opposition and sin; but the reality of heaven and hell was unquestioned. God was not a mere hypothesis without which the world could not be adequately accounted for, nor the devil an outmoded *façon de parler*. The terrestrial hierarchy was a reflection of the celestial, from which it drew both its form and its justification. Whenever questions arose, the authority of tradition rather than the ingenuity of man was looked to to supply the answer.

Only quite recently has a contrary point of view gained ascendancy; the simplest name for it is the profane point of view. It is anti-traditional, progressive, humanist, rationalist, materialist, experimental, individualist, egalitarian, free-thinking and intensely sentimental. Such a point of view has always existed in one form or another. What is new is its dominance. Now practically worldwide, it dominates almost every domain of human life and thought.

To get a fully adequate picture of a very complex and comprehensive situation it would be necessary to take account of many other of its aspects; for instance, how the scientistic attitude persuades man that he is master of his own destiny; or how, as the mainspring of industry, it destroys the kind of work that is natural and necessary to man.[1] It would be necessary to consider how profane philosophy, sharing the outlook of science, creates inextricable confusion by trying to find the answer to the most crucial of all questions, 'What am I', where it is not to be found, namely in the human brain (for the eye cannot see itself).[2] It would be necessary to consider how art is the mirror of its times, and from being purely symbolical becomes purely aesthetic;[3] and the parts played by literature, entertainment and advertising in changing human nature.[4] All these things and many more are integral parts of the same picture. They are by no means unconnected with its religious aspect. But we are not for the moment concerned so much with things that oppose Religion with secularism or materialism of various kinds, nor with things that merely distract attention from Religion. We are concerned with things that attack it in the first place by doing all they can to sap the sources of its strength, and in the second place by setting up against it many kinds of more or less plausible counterfeits.

The profane point of view applied to Religion has caused everything not susceptible of direct proof based on the evidence of the senses to be called in question. Many things that are by their nature not accessible to the understanding of the masses have been set aside; yet these things tend to be the intellectual elements that are really fundamental. The result is the growing prevalence of a Religion that is reduced to its third element, the ethical or moral.

With the weakening of the directing influence of the more intellectual elements everything tends increasingly towards a mere sentimental humanism, confined in its outlook to the things of this world, and therefore defenseless against the assaults of its enemies. It becomes a Religion without mystery, denuded of most of its essentials. Nothing greater than man remains. Very soon happiness rather than salvation becomes the biggest good and the final goal, and pain

1. Chap. 5, p36.
2. Chap. 7, p57.
3. Chap. 6, p45.
4. Chap. 8, p63.

rather than damnation becomes the greatest evil and the ultimate dread. It is scarcely too much to say that Religion has then virtually ceased to be Religion, although it still professes a belief in God.

It is not surprising that a Religion thus attenuated fails to satisfy either the instinctively felt needs of the masses, or the minds of many who are intelligent enough to perceive its weakness.

Human inadequacy in no way affects the truth, which remains what it was and always will be. Truth being what it is, it necessarily reaches us through the superhuman channel of Revelation, and not through the purely human one of discovery.

We are indeed a long way from the strength and purity of the original Revelation. The chain of Tradition which links us to it has been greatly strained, but until it is completely broken a renewal is always possible. Religion has been grossly sentimentalized and humanized, distorted and even perverted, and sometimes reduced to little more than a kind of idealism or ideology competing with profane ideologies for the same ends, an alternative way of promoting welfare. One can say without exaggeration that today the Kingdom of God frequently appears to be envisaged as little more than a full realization of the ideals of the welfare state.

It is a fact, however, that no such ideals can command for long the natural loyalty of men, which tends towards what is above themselves and not to what is on their own level. In practice that means towards whatever in their civilization most nearly, or most accessibly, represents the supernatural, to Tradition in general and to a hierarchical superior in particular. The secret longing of man— hidden sometimes even from himself—is to serve God. When no satisfactory opportunity to do so, even indirectly, comes to him from his environment, when nobody tells him how to seek it but on the contrary every influence urges him to seek something else, his secret longing remains unsatisfied and he loses his sense of loyalty and of purpose.

Communism and other subversive movements know very well that a Religion identified with ideals of welfare has lost its *raison d'être* and is at their mercy. Things have gone a long way in that direction when it becomes necessary to point out that the end of Religion is not welfare but salvation, and that 'faith in human nature' or 'faith in the future' have nothing whatever to do with faith in God. If the attainment of salvation is the true purpose of human life, in what way does a mere raising of the standard of living contribute to the attainment of that purpose, if meanwhile faith in God decays?

It is as if the world were the scene of the development of a gigantic plot to turn man away from God, in the first place by eliminating Tradition, which is the vehicle of Religion because it is a perpetuation of Revelation. The plot is in fact just as real as the devil is.[5] In the achievement of the objective of this plot the propagation of the notion of progress, or progressive evolution, has hitherto occupied a central position. As applied to Religion it carries the implication that Religion itself progresses as it were automatically, so that it tends to get better or purer as time goes on, and therefore that a modernized Religion is likely to be an improvement on an ancient one. This notion contradicts all that is implicit in the notion of the completeness and sufficiency of the original Revelation, and of the main duty of man being to lose as little as possible of that completeness through the lapse of time.

The maintenance of a true Religion is not compatible with the profane point of view, or, to give it another name, the modernistic outlook. Whenever attempts are made to accommodate Religion to the modernistic outlook (in its scientific dress or otherwise) the result is inevitably a denaturing of Religion. This often includes a rejection or ignoring of everything in the Sacred Scriptures which does not fit in with the new outlook, and the substitution of the kind of 'gospel of wellbeing' already mentioned, which situates heaven in a terrestrial future and abolishes hell.

But it is not necessary to adopt the modernistic outlook simply because one is alive today. Even though it be almost impossible to maintain a traditional outlook in all phases of life today, it is still possible and even vitally necessary to do so in Religion. It is for this reason that Religion must nowadays be kept in a distinct domain, more or less apart from the secular domain, despite the disadvantages of any such separation. These disadvantages spring from the

5. Chap. 3, pp 23–25.

fact that there is strictly speaking nothing, not even such things as are undiluted manifestations of the profane point of view, that has nothing to do with Religion, simply because there is nothing that has nothing to do with God. Everything is either affirmation or denial of Him. Therefore to think of anything as being entirely detached from Religion is to ignore its most essential relationships.[6]

The propagation of the notion of progressive evolution is one of the many lines of attack that can be broadly grouped under the heading of materialism. It is not sufficient however from the point of view of the enemies of God merely to undermine religious faith by the propagation of materialism in one form or another, in order to divert attention from faith to the attractions of the world. The attractiveness of earthly things is apt to fade; the devil knows well enough that they can never be satisfying for long, and that the bait has to be changed with growing frequency. When materialism has done most of its work and is beginning to be called in question as its results show themselves to be increasingly unsatisfactory, people's minds begin to turn back towards Religion. But by then many have forgotten what Religion is. They get no help from their environment. Many no doubt turn back towards orthodoxy, but many more turn towards one of the innumerable pseudo-religious movements, sects and cults which are increasingly taking the place of orthodox Religion. In many of these movements some of the outward characteristics of Religion are preserved. In some cases those characteristics that would usually be regarded as interior or esoteric are more or less closely imitated. Some are 'sects' in the sense that ostensibly they are not detached from their parent Religion. Practically all of their adherents are well-meaning and guileless—that is the tragedy of the situation—but the same cannot always be said of their originators and leaders.

These pseudo-religious movements, sects and cults are by far the most insidious enemies of Religion. They can fill the vacuum caused by its absence without fulfilling its essential purpose. Being

---

6. It then becomes impossible to situate it correctly in the scheme of things. Nevertheless this may be a lesser evil than that of falsifying the nature of Religion, in circumstances such as the present, when one or the other is inevitable.

inventions and not traditions, whatever claim to orthodoxy or to inspiration they may make, they can never be a means of grace. On the contrary, at best they are totally ineffectual, and at worst there is no limit to the harm they can do, not so much to body or mind, though that can be great, but to the immortal soul.[7]

The neglect or denial of Religion is one thing; its distortion or perversion is another. The former is at least straightforward and unequivocal; it leaves the soul empty. The latter is subtle and confusing; it fills the soul with poison. There is no real defense against it other than an unswerving, wholehearted and uncompromising attachment to an orthodox Religion. Therefore what matters most is to know at least in principle what orthodox Religion is. It then becomes unnecessary to try to sort out the conflicting claims of the pseudo-religions.

It is impossible to overstress the seriousness of the danger that pseudo-religions represent. The world is obsessed by fear, but it is a fear of things that can destroy only the body, and it takes little or no account of things that can first distort and then destroy the soul. There is no comparison between the two objects of fear, for heaven and hell are more real than this ephemeral world of appearances and illusions.

✠

Religious people, and particularly those who practice some kind of austerity, are sometimes accused of being concerned only with saving their own souls instead of doing good to others, as if they were doing something selfish or contrary to Christian charity. Nothing could be more absurd. Does Christianity really place terrestrial welfare above salvation? No man can save any soul but his own. How could anyone who has no experience of the way towards salvation hope to show it to anyone else, or even to avoid obstructing him? One who is good cannot help doing good. One who is not good

---

7. Chap. 9, p78.

cannot hope to do good whatever he does. The effect of every act, whether charitable in intention or not, is dependent on the 'intent' of the doer, that is, on the direction in which his soul is oriented. If the intent is right, even a natural and unimportant act (such as giving a cup of cold water) will do good. If the intent is not right, even an outwardly charitable act will be turned towards evil. So the most charitable of all acts, the act without which no other act can be charitable, is one which is directed towards the saving of the only soul for which the doer is responsible.

But there is something more important still. Every spiritual act is done on behalf of humanity. It contributes to the fulfillment of the purpose for which man was created—that of keeping the world in touch with God and bringing it back to Him. Only in the spiritual act is man fully human, and without it every act is undertaken in vain.

This life is not an end in itself. It is not justified by its pleasantness, nor by its length, but only insofar as it serves to purify and perfect the soul, and to make that soul ready to meet its God, as it must. The only certainty in life is death. It could even be said that the only reality in life is death, for the reality of the world of appearances is not its own, and death is the moment when the veil of the flesh is torn away and we see the reality that lies behind it. We see it then not as now 'through a glass, darkly,' but 'face to face' (1 Cor. 13:12).

The immense reality of death and its significance seem to be lost to this generation, which has forgotten that it is not the fact of death that is a cause for concern, nor the time of its occurrence, but the readiness of the soul to meet it.

Even if everything that has been said so far is accepted, doubt may still remain as to how to apply it to a particular case—one's own for instance.

The guidance offered from sources claiming orthodoxy is often conflicting or vague or unconvincing. The guidance offered from other sources is still more conflicting and inevitably lacks authority. How pleasant it would be if one could offer a simple prescription suitable for anyone, thus putting an end to doubts and hesitations! But applications to particular cases cannot be dealt with without taking into consideration the qualifications and situation of the individual concerned. For that reason anything that can be said here must be in very general terms.

The important thing about any statement is not whether it is general or particular, but whether it is true or untrue. Unless the truth can be grasped in its broad essentials it is unlikely that specific action will be soundly based. In the end, therefore, everyone must seek for himself the application appropriate to himself.

His search is much more likely to be fruitful if he has some idea what he is looking for. If he is looking for a new Religion there is one thing to make quite sure about first, and that is whether what he already has may not after all be what he is looking for. Even if he is sure that it is not exactly that, it may still be the nearest practicable approach to it, and therefore something not to be lightly thrown to the winds. He must be sure that what he is looking for may not after all be discoverable there where he is rather than elsewhere.

God will not refuse His guidance to one who seeks it with humility, perseverance, patience and confidence. He often allows us to be led astray for a time so that we may understand what is wrong; or to be confused for a time so as to test our real intention. Victory may not come till the last moment; it may come when least expected and in the most unexpected form.

God knows well how difficult things are at this time. He 'trieth not a soul beyond its capacity.'[8]

8. Koran 2:286.

3

THE IDEA OF GOD

EVERYONE likes to think that he has a clear idea of what he is talking about. This implies being able to define it more or less precisely, and to fit it into some kind of category.

Definition and classification are tendencies inherent in thought itself. They are perfectly valid as a means of reducing the complexity of phenomena to some kind of intelligible order; but they are not applicable in the same degree to everything. Their applicability or otherwise to anything is by no means a measure of its relative importance or of its reality, as is so often assumed.

The fact that thought encounters objects which it cannot get hold of and cannot fit into a preconceived category does not affect the nature of those objects; it is simply a measure of the natural limitations of thought. Among such objects are some of the least important and least real things in life, like commonplace dreams and fantasies; but also some of the most important and most real, like beauty, goodness and love, and most important of all, as comprehending all three and much more also, what may, for want of a better term, be called the idea of God.

There is no greater mistake than mentally to group all these things together, the least real with the most real, the ill-defined with the undefinable, and to brand them all as mere subjective notions, having a more or less accidental relevance to the hard facts of ordinary life, and to do so simply on account of their common non-systematic character and their refusal to conform to the limitative and classificatory tendencies of thought. The validity of a conception resides in its conformity to the nature of its object. A naturally non-systematic object demands a conception of a similar character. Such a conception, where it is appropriate, will be much more precise than one which is forced into a preconceived category.

We are thinking beings. To exclude God from our thoughts would be to exclude Him from our lives. Yet owing to the limited capacities and restrictive tendencies of thought, we cannot hope to think of Him as He is. We must think of Him as we can, namely, in terms of His qualities or attributes, but inevitably more or less distinctively, systematically and even anthropomorphically, as we do when we think of Him as Infinite, Absolute or Eternal, or as Truth, Love or Majesty, or as Creator, Preserver or Judge. All these terms, together with an indefinite number of others possible, are limitative. Even the words infinite, absolute and eternal are mutually limitative, for if they were not so they would be one word, not three.

No distinctive conception of God can have an exclusive validity, and God is greater than the sum of all possible conceptions.

Nevertheless the distinctive and multiple conceptions enumerated above, as well as many others, are established and sanctified by Tradition; they are adapted to the nature and the needs of man, and as such are necessary and providential. So far from being obstacles to a realization of the Unicity and Unity of the Infinite, they represent necessary steps towards it, but by a process of synthesis rather than one of addition. Individual conceptions having no traditional sanction are not in the same category.

We tend to look for a mental satisfaction of the kind that can arise from grasping an idea and tidying it away in a mental compartment. What we need is a mental discipline, and that is what the traditional conceptions of Divinity can supply, on condition that their synthesis is made possible by an integration with the Religion to which they belong. The mind is not the whole of man, and the mental image is less than the mind. In order to form a mental image adequate to the representation of Divinity, man would have to be greater than God. If we insist on forming a mental image which we can regard as adequate and exclusive, then the object of that image is not God but merely some figment of our imagination.

Nevertheless man alone of all beings can be conscious of God, independently of the intervention of distinctive thoughts and words.

The very few in whom that consciousness has become total are not as other men. For the vast majority of mankind consciousness takes the form of what we call belief or faith in God. Such belief is therefore not something primitive or childish or vague, or fit only for those who have nothing better, as it is so often represented to be today. It is, on the contrary, for most of us our closest link with truth; it is a manifestation of a consciousness of reality, whether it be clear and strong or confused and weak. When it is clear and strong it merges into vision and, like vision, it then has no need of thoughts or of words. In its simplicity and strength, belief may come nearer to its object than the subtlest thoughts or the most impeccable of dissertations; it goes straight to the fountainhead, bypassing all conceptual elaborations.

Here we come back in a circle, for we cannot escape from conceptual elaborations: they are part of our makeup. We must form some image of God; one could say that, being made as we are, we are meant to form some image of God, or rather a series of partial images, the succession of which, since they can only be formed one at a time, beguiles the soul in the direction of the single vision of God. The imagery which Tradition presents to us for our meditation symbolizes the Unity of Divinity and is at the same time adapted to our multiplicity; it is a matrix or system of compatibles or compossibles that are many, but can be seen or realized as one.

A system as such is by definition limited in that it excludes other possible systems, whatever may be its potentialities in the direction of universality, so that no single system could be expected to be adapted to the needs of a world composed of very varied and more or less narrow-minded peoples. Hence the multiplicity of Traditions, each unique and self-sufficient in principle, but each offering what appears on the surface to be a different idea of God. There is no reason why the components of any one system should normally fit into another.

The imagery presented by the various Traditions is not only in itself multiple, but is also different in each case, often to the point of apparent incomparability, especially in its more outward aspects. For instance, the multiple aspect of Divinity is presented in Christianity in the first place in the doctrine of the Trinity, as well is in the attributes that have scriptural sanction, such as the Way, the Truth, the Light, etc.; in Hinduism by what may appear to a Christian as a mere multiplication of deities, the interior coherence of that Tradition not being easily observable from without. The case of the Traditions of Greece and Rome is comparable at least in their original forms (the question of the degree to which they eventually became really polytheistic being left in abeyance); in Mahayana Buddhism it is presented by the indefinite multiplication of Buddhas and Bodhisattvas; in Islam, itself essentially a doctrine of Unity, by the Divine Names, each representing a Divine quality or attribute, and indefinite in number.

Imagery, moreover, can be of several kinds, notably mental, visual, auditive and sensorial. As an integration of the whole human personality is in question all must be provided for and none can be inherently invalid. These four categories can be most directly and broadly exemplified by, first, the idea that seeks expression in words; second, the statue or picture or building; third, music, and in addition certain recitations and formulae; and fourth, the dance. They are of course often combined, as in poetry or ceremonial or drama.

Every Tradition normally provides in some way for the integration of all four categories of imagery, but emphasis differs. For instance, among Europeans in general the idea takes precedence, whereas among the Negro races it is the dance. Visual imagery takes a prominent place in Mahayana Buddhism, and the auditive among many nomadic peoples. The idea is more complex than the other three, but less direct, which is no doubt why it predominates among Europeans with their predominantly cerebral inclinations. It is not for that or any other reason necessarily more effective in leading men towards the vision of God.

All these things and more can be effective in leading men to God, but they can also become idols; and they inevitably do so when their symbolical significance has been lost. When their power has passed from them, they become superstitions in the real sense of the word, namely 'things left over'.

It is as absurd to maintain that a statue is necessarily an idol as it is to maintain that an idea never is so. It is as absurd to say that the dance can never be a means of grace as it would be to say that music always is so. The sacred or idolatrous character of a thing depends not so much on its external form as on the use that is made of it.[1]

✠

It has been said that one who does not believe in the devil does not believe in God. The sense in which this statement is true can be explained in several ways, of which the following is one. It starts from the assumption that to say that someone believes something is equivalent to saying that he thinks it is real.

There is one logically inescapable conception, and it is that of infinity, of that which has no limit of any kind. It is impossible to conceive of an absolute limit, for it would have to be as it were a one-sided boundary, a door having an inside face but no outside face. There is no limit unless there is something beyond it. There can be no possibility, whether it be realized or not, that is outside infinity. This conception is fundamental in metaphysical science.

Affirmation and negation are both possibilities. Infinity, which alone cannot not be, affirms itself in us as personal God, we being persons, while itself it is neither personal nor impersonal since both are indications. The possibility of its negation appears as the negation of the personal God, which we personify as the devil or Satan.

If God is thus regarded as pure affirmation it would seem that the devil should represent pure negation: but pure negation is not possible, because negation exists only by virtue of what it denies. It has no independent reality, but only a reality derived from the reality of that which it denies. If God is really, from a certain point of view, personal, the personification of the devil is justified by his relation

1. Nevertheless the idolatrous use of a form can leave its mark on that form, or on certain manifestations of it, up to the point at which those manifestations can no longer be effective as means of grace, but only as instruments of subversion. The idolatrous and subversive character of much of the music now in vogue is, to some people at least, self-evident, and much the same can be said about the other arts. Such manifestations can properly be said to be diabolical or satanic, in that they are examples of the turning of means normally good to evil ends.

to God, negative though it be. But it would be the greatest mistake to suppose that for that or any other reason the devil is wholly unreal. On the contrary, negation is a very real, and not merely a hypothetical possibility. This fact is a measure of the reality of the devil, which, however, has nothing absolute about it, like the Reality of God. But the devil is real enough on the relative plane, which is that on which we find ourselves, even though on that, as on all other planes, pure negation, the denial of nothing, is meaningless and void. Negation seeks to abolish that which it denies; but if it is successful it simultaneously abolishes itself, as it has no intrinsic reality, but only a borrowed reality. The devil, as being the personified negation of the personal God, draws his reality (always relative) from God (who alone is absolute Reality); if he were to be so successful as to forget what it is that he is denying, he would cease to be.

Thus the devil is his own worst enemy, but meanwhile he is ours also, and if God works through us, the devil works through us too. Only when the sense of the immanent reality of God in the world becomes excessively weakened does the devil manage to hide or disguise himself by pretending that he too has little or no reality, thereby eliminating man's natural and proper fear of himself.

To resume: no imagery, no representation of God and no formulation of the idea of God can by itself or by virtue of its form alone communicate truth unequivocally to all. On the other hand a traditional imagery or formulation, even if it appears to exclude other traditional formulations, can provide all that is necessary, subject to two conditions: firstly the support of the traditional framework appropriate to itself, and secondly the sincerity and right intent of whoever accepts and makes use of it.

The true intent of a soul is known to God alone. The Day of Judgment will bring many surprises. We Europeans are apt to underrate the virtues of simplicity and directness, and to mistake complexity for profundity, judging the intent of others accordingly. When Traditions were more or less isolated there was less room for misjudgment than there is now. Today everyone is on everyone else's doorstep, if not inside his house, so that the natural and inevitable incompatibilities between Traditions are forced upon us, and added to the already excessive internal divisions and complications of our own. The idea of God appropriate to Christianity does indeed differ in its outward form and imagery from that of other Traditions; but questions concerning those differences are of much less significance for Europeans than the question of how far the Christian idea has retained its original purity and comprehensiveness, or how far it has become restricted and distorted.[2]

An assumption underlying much of what has been said so far on this subject is that there are degrees or planes of reality. It has for instance been suggested that dreams and fantasies are less real than the great and universal qualities of beauty, goodness and love. Few are likely to disagree. Not everyone however would agree at once that our existence here on earth has a degree of reality that lies somewhere between the two. Yet it is we who produce the dreams and fantasies, whereas nothing we can do can affect the qualities, which remain eternally what they are. They may be manifested in and through us, either by way of affirmation or of negation, but always temporarily and never perfectly. They are on a higher plane of reality than our ephemeral and imperfect existence. What then of Him who comprehends them all and much more also, not in any sense as their sum, but as their common principle of excellence?

There is no discontinuity between the planes of reality; they are therefore indefinite in number. Traditionally they are represented in various ways, in the multiple heavens of Judaism and of Dante, in the storeyed structure of the Hindu temple, in the angelology of several Traditions, and so on. Their continuity implies that while a higher plane can never be described in terms of a lower, yet the lower is always a symbol of the higher and as such can suggest or evoke it. Thus, on the terrestrial plane, everything is a symbol of the

---

2. There are no doubt still some Christians whose idea of God corresponds to a picture of a handsome old man in voluminous robes ensconced in a cloud. Childish perhaps, but is it less realistic, or even less anthropomorphic, than many current quasi-philosophical, psychological or ultra-sentimental representations?

higher reality from which it derives its own degree of reality, as it were by reflection or refraction. Some things reflect the higher reality more directly and more affirmatively than others. First among such things are the symbols presented to us by Tradition: they above all things can lead men by way of the ascending series of planes of reality towards the vision of the absolute Reality of God.

4

Tradition & Anti-Tradition

TRADITION, in the rightful sense of the word, is the chain that joins civilization to Revelation. It comprises all the distinctive characteristics that make any given civilization what it is, including those that can more specifically be called religious. Every Divine Revelation has inaugurated not only a new Religion, but also a new civilization, each with its own particular advantages and limitations, its own genius, its own point of view and its own arts and sciences.

Tradition and civilization are not mere accidents of time and place, nor are they human inventions, nor yet mere mechanical responses to environment, that is to say, products of evolution in the modern scientific sense of the word. A Tradition once established does indeed evolve; it has a history covering its rise, the development to maturity of its full potentialities, and its eventual decay. Tradition could be said to make history rather than to be made by history. Its origin is the kind of direct divine intervention we call Revelation, and all its potentialities are present, though not manifested, at its inception.

The existence of Traditions and, above all, their qualities, cannot be accounted for by any man-made theory, and certainly not by the theory of evolution for which Darwin is commonly held responsible.

Each Tradition has as it were an individuality of its own and a perfection of its own, which is however always relative. Thus the world is enriched as it could not be if all civilizations were the same, or if all men were of the same type. The Revelations are, so to speak, adapted to the peoples to whom they were sent, and to the circumstances prevailing at the time of their appearance. The Koran says: 'If he had so willed, God would have made you all one people'; also: 'God has sent to every people a Messenger speaking their own language.' And so it is.

The individuality and the relative perfection of each Tradition is particularly evident in the field of the arts, which may be taken as an example. Though in most cases a traditional art is an adaptation and a revitalization of a pre-existing art, it always acquires a new inspiration both precious and distinctive, and to a certain extent incomparable. The Far-Eastern, Hindu, Christian and Islamic civilizations have all produced what may generically be called temples; yet the Chinese and Indian temples, the cathedral and the mosque regarded as expressions of beauty are both mutually and absolutely incomparable, like the beauty of the lily and the rose. The same applies to their productions in other branches of art. Individual preferences are of course legitimate and normal but do not affect the reality. Is an image of the Buddha more beautiful or less beautiful than an icon? The question is meaningless.

The chain of Tradition is usually considered in its historical, temporal or 'horizontal' aspect, though it also has a social, spatial or 'vertical' aspect. In its historical aspect it is a real spiritual heredity, the continuity of which is preserved by the initiatic transmission of a function to each individual from his predecessor. We are familiar with a sacred or initiatic transmission of function in the case of priests and kings, and as a matter of history in the case of certain crafts, particularly that of building. In a fully traditional civilization a comparable kind of transmission exists, in many different outward forms, in respect of every essential function in the community. It ensures the effective integration of each function with the providential pattern of the civilization in question, so that there is nothing that is not sacred, at least in principle, and the words spiritual heredity have a real meaning.

There is indeed a close analogy with physical heredity, the continuity of which is unquestionable. Physical heredity is the basis of the unity of the family and the race, which exist only for so long as their hereditary continuity is unbroken. A break in that continuity is final: it can by no conceivable means be repaired; a family that has died out has died out forever. It is cut off from its origin. Anything that may replace it is not the same family, whatever it may be called. The rupture of a spiritual heredity can be no less final, and for a comparable reason, namely, a break in the chain of tradition.

The chain of Tradition in its social or vertical aspect appears as the hierarchy of functions which unifies the collectivity, much as the various organs of a single living creature are unified by their subordination one to another, as well as by their interdependence. A firmly established hierarchy of functions is a condition of unity and vitality in a civilization; it forms a chain that links the highest to the lowest, as well as a chain that links the past with the future. In such a society a man's function is more important than his individual character. Without an established function man can be neither useful nor content. Where such a hierarchy exists most people will exercise their function through service to a hierarchical superior, who is regarded, not so much as an individual, but as the holder for the time being of an office necessary to the maintenance of the coherence of the civilization, and as representing a link in the chain through which the spiritual influence descends and gives life to all. The effective continuity of the chain is independent of the fact that the holder of a particular office may sometimes, as an individual, be unworthy of his position. Thus the humblest function is integrated with the whole, and every man can feel, though it be but subconsciously, that his work is justified by something greater than its tangible results.

Such, very briefly stated, are the principles which have governed the course of human life throughout by far the greater part of history. That is not to say that it would be possible to point to a civilization, past or present, in which they have been perfectly followed, since nothing human is perfect. There have always been errors, failures, abuses and sin. But, even if there were no errors, evil in the sense of hardship, pain and death would still be present, because they are implicit in terrestrial existence. That existence, at least since the fall of man, is essentially a manifestation of the separation of good and evil, which itself is an aspect of the separation of affirmation and negation already mentioned. Hardship, pain and the death of the body are therefore inevitable, but they are lesser evils because they are tied to time, whereas damnation is not so. Moreover hardship and pain can be expiatory, and death can be sacrificial, so that all three can become instruments of that greater good we call salvation.

Pain as expiation, death as sacrifice; how remote and incomprehensible are such notions to the modern mind! Yet our ancestors— and not so very long ago either—knew that the law of compensation is universal, and that suffering is necessary, and that it is better to suffer in this world than in the next.

Comparisons between civilizations are of no value unless they are based on valid criteria. It is often difficult to assess the degree to which any given civilization is or has been effective as a framework for the spiritual development of its members, or as a support to them on the road to salvation: yet this is the final and only fully valid criterion. The criteria of institutional stability and individual contentment are not valueless, but they are secondary. Standard of living in the modern sense of the words has no importance whatever.

One thing however is evident. Modern civilization is built on a very different foundation, one in which standard of living has become the only criterion that is taken seriously. Tradition, Religion and everything else are subordinated to that point of view, to which the epithet 'profane' is entirely appropriate, since its derivation relates to those who stand outside the sacred precinct.

In order to avoid possible misunderstanding it may be desirable to point out, so far as standard of living is concerned and in parenthesis, that life in a traditional civilization by no means implies any kind of puritanical abstention from the good things of this world just because they are pleasurable. They are indeed good only because they reflect on a lower plane a greater and more durable good. That being so, it should be evident that if they are sought for their own sake and as if mankind enjoyed them by right and not by grace, and without the acknowledgment of their source implicit in a traditional way of life,[1] they become idols and the souls of men are bound to the lower plane and can never rise above it. Their gaze is

---

1. Acknowledgement of that source, whatever form it may take, always involves some kind of sacrifice either of the good things themselves or in the lives of those who enjoy them.

as it were turned downwards and not upwards. They can only come to know what is beneath them and not what is above them—hell and not heaven.

The change of point of view from traditional to profane really originates in a gradual restriction of the field of vision, associated with the centrifugal tendency of all manifestation, exemplified in time by the evident fact that everything gets progressively farther from its origin. The result is a kind of myopia limited in its range to the world of sensorial perceptions. What is claimed as greatly increased knowledge of the universe is in fact confined to a relatively unimportant aspect of that universe, namely its outward appearance. From this restricted point of view we can learn only what it looks like to us and not what it is. Not that this view is wholly subjective; it is in fact to a certain extent objective, but very incompletely so; it is objective only insofar as the reality of the universe coincides with the highly particularized effects it produces on our senses; whether those senses be aided or unaided makes no difference.

Some people believe in extra-sensory perception, but if such a thing is possible it is still perception, still limited by our earthly form and coinciding with reality only as far as that form permits.

There is almost a kind of willfulness about all this, a deliberate relegation to a subsidiary position of everything that is above the plane of earthly existence. There is a calculated rejection of the celestial in favor of the terrestrial in almost all we do, if not in all we say. The fact is that, willfully or not, we no longer in general see heaven and hell as realities, nor do we sense that reality of which all visible things are but shadows. The profane point of view is therefore highly unrealistic, though it prides itself on its realism. The propagandists of modern science foster the delusion that science is in the process of revealing the real nature of the universe, with the implication that the kind of Revelation postulated by Religion is less realistic, or at least less practically important. In fact the latter comprehends the profane view and puts it into its proper and rightful place.

The two points of view situate the ultimate reality of things at two opposite poles—matter and the Spirit. Consequently in every field of thought and activity they are in conflict. For instance, from the traditional point of view, the history of the world had a divine beginning and must therefore also have a divine end, a Day of Judgment, so that history is cyclical and not continuous nor of indefinite extent. From the profane point of view history is regarded as indefinite, without beginning and without end, like a boundless matrix filled with events and things of varying but always relative importance. No place can be found for notions of creation or Revelation or Judgment.

In the first case the reality of the world is contingent on the superior reality of a Creator, Preserver, and a Judge; in the second case time and space and their contents alone are real and everything else, including the truths of Religion, is conjectural. In the first case there is an absolute Truth, reflected more directly in Religion than in anything else, so that only certain applications of it are matters of opinion; in the second case all truth is relative, and there is nothing except that which can be directly observed and measured which is not a matter of opinion. In the first case a man normally allows his Tradition to think for him to a greater or lesser extent, relying on a wisdom that is postulated to be the divinely ordained source of his Tradition. In the second every man must think for himself, at least to the extent of choosing whom of his fellow men he will allow to think for him, so that there is no guidance more reliable than that proceeding from the activity of the human brain, despite the fact that the results of that activity, in the form of the opinions of the philosophers, scientists or experts are as varied and conflicting as are the opinions of those who look to them for guidance.

Traditionally the story of mankind is the story of a descent from an Edenic state accompanied by the possibility of a reascent; modernistically it is the story of a progress from a primitive or backward to an advanced state. It is difficult to exaggerate the extent of the changes in contemporary thought and activity attributable to this particular inversion of outlook. Traditionally man is an instrument in the hands of God; modernistically he is an independent being in control of his own destiny. Thus he puts himself in the place of God, both as the orderer of his own life and also as one to whom all service is due.

Tradition sees the hand of God in everything; modernism sees nothing but blind forces.

Such, very briefly, is the fundamental change of outlook that has taken place. As to its effects, they are everywhere for anyone who cares to see. They are seen in the development of modern industry, with its destruction of that pride of function or craftsmanship in which the most important objective is the perfection of the work and only second the reward it may bring. They are seen in that inevitable corollary of industry, namely, advertising, which keeps industry going by an artificial and antispiritual stimulation of desire for more and more possessions and distractions, besides affording a readily available channel for subtler propaganda. In art, where a desire to escape from the boredom of a purely profane reproduction of nature leads to the exaltation of infantilism and psychopathic distortion. And not least in politics, wherein the democratic idea replaces the hierarchical, and power is, at least in theory, put into the hands of those who collectively and by definition embody the average intelligence.[2]

The enumeration of contrasts between the two points of view could be pursued indefinitely, for there is virtually nothing in our daily lives that is not affected by the choice made between them. The change from one to the other has taken place step by step; some steps have been gradual and some abrupt, and they have not coincided everywhere, so that it is not possible to say that the profane point of view attained to predominance at one moment and not at another. The one thing certain is that its predominance is now almost ubiquitous, and that it has become almost total in some parts of the world.

2. Incidentally this is not even common sense. Aristocracy is the only common sense, provided that it really is government by the best, and that the best really have the right qualifications. The power of the average is in any case always ineffectual because it is inevitably dominated by something less mediocre than itself, either, as in a traditional civilization, by intelligences hierarchically ordered in an upward direction, or, where for one reason or another the hierarchical organization has ceased to be effective, by any intelligence that has the desire and the ability to dominate, whatever may be its objectives, and whether or not it allows or persuades the collectivity to think that it wields the effective power.

Tradition alone, as the chain that binds man to God, affords real protection from the greater evil—the evil that is most to be feared because it is permanent. In compensation, since perfection is not realizable on earth, Tradition imposes constraints of certain kinds— disciplines if you like; and further, it does not attempt any kind of earthly perfectionism, knowing that any such attempt is unpractical and that it diverts attention from the 'one thing needful'.

Modernism, with its shortsighted earthly perfectionism, leaves no room for the pursuit of the greater good; it scorns the protection offered by Tradition, thereby leaving the way open to the greater evil.

If this is indeed the situation, why is it not more clearly seen and more widely accepted? Its existence has been attributed earlier to a restriction of the field of vision, whereby the truth becomes less and less clearly perceived. This however need not imply that when the truth is pointed out it still cannot be perceived; yet experience shows that this can happen. There is indeed another and tougher obstacle, and it is precisely the scornfulness just mentioned. Its other name is pride, the pride that thinks that its achievements are so great that it has no need to ask for forgiveness and mercy; that it can quite well look after itself.

Someone will say: 'But surely God intended us to use the faculties He gave us?' Yes indeed; but to use them in the way laid down by Him and to use them in His service, not in our own.

5

MODERN
SCIENCE

FAITH in modern science is now firmly established. Insofar as it has recently come to be questioned in some quarters, it is almost entirely on the grounds that the new possibilities opened up are liable to misuse, and not on the grounds of any inherent insufficiency in the modern scientific outlook.

The words 'modern science' are used here in preference to the word 'science' alone, though to most of our contemporaries they would mean the same thing. The qualification is however very important. There have been and still are other sciences, no less exact, but built up on very different foundations. They comprise, broadly speaking, the various branches of the traditional science. Their foundation is to a greater or lesser degree metaphysical; this aspect of their nature will be returned to shortly. Of most of them only a few distorted and often perverted relics remain.

Before proceeding further it is desirable to state clearly that adverse criticism of the modern scientific point of view does not imply adverse criticism of every scientific worker as an individual, so long, of course, as he does his work conscientiously.

The outlook which has produced modern science in fact pervades almost everything that anyone can find to do today, whether his work be specifically scientific in the restricted sense of the word or not. Whether a person's work is scientific or not is largely a matter of what we usually call chance, that is to say, of the individual's heritage (or the destiny that he is) and his environment (the destiny that he meets). He did not choose either. Nevertheless the relative freedom man enjoys implies that he can choose to some extent what he makes of his twofold destiny.[1]

Modern science, together with the philosophy and the industry that are organically one with it, is the expression *par excellence* in our civilization of the profane point of view. Its outlook is in principle and in practice confined to things that can be observed, described and, as nearly as their nature permits, measured.

Modern science has two objectives: to arrive at a description of the observable universe (which includes the human body and mind) in the hope that its real nature will become increasingly apparent, and to make use of the knowledge acquired so as to enable man to exercise an ever increasing control over his environment, and so to find ways of doing, making or obtaining things more economically or more abundantly. The two objectives (roughly those of pure and applied science) often overlap either by accident or by design. They are both pursued by means of research, which includes direct observation and the observation of the results of experiments. From the accumulated observations, generalizations or hypotheses are constructed which, especially in popular language, are often called theories.[2] In this way a picture of the observable universe is built up and an ever-growing flood of innovations is introduced into the daily life of the community.

Modern science has indeed amassed a vast quantity of information about the observable universe, and the effects of its innovations

1. Whether he simply does as well as he can whatever his hand finds to do, or whether he chooses to become, for instance, one of the popularizers of modern science (or of what will pass as such with the general public), or one of those who try to elevate their philosophy of science to a position not only equal to that of traditional philosophy but even above it. Any assumption of authority, except in the purely technical field, involves the assumption of a responsibility that cannot be evaded.

2. Here it may be pointed out in parenthesis that the word 'theory' has two distinct meanings: one is the modern meaning just mentioned, namely, the construction of generalizations, sometimes wrongly referred to as principles, from the assembly and study of observed and recorded facts; the other is the ancient and original meaning, namely, the understanding of observed facts in the light of principles established and handed down by Tradition.

on everyday life have indeed been revolutionary. Nevertheless every scientist would acknowledge the incompleteness of the picture of the universe so far formed and the provisional nature of the results attained. He would probably also claim that the results arrived at so far represent an approach to truth, and that they have operated, or must ultimately operate, for the good of mankind.

The knowledge acquired and the postulates arrived at do not however necessarily represent an approach to truth. They depend upon the assumption that there is nothing of critical importance inaccessible to observation or to deduction from observation. There are obviously two obstacles to such an assumption. The first is the observer himself and the second is God.

The observer is by definition other than the observed, so that he can never fully observe himself. In addition he can observe nothing that is outside his potentialities as an observer (such things will not exist for him). This is a crucial point.

Chapter 3 was concerned with the idea of God and His inaccessibility to observation, and nothing more need be added here, except to say that when attention is confined to the observable, the observable tends increasingly to be equated with the real. The notion of a reality too great to be observable slips into the background and is finally suppressed. In the end, since neither the observer nor God can be fitted into the system, they are either ignored or turned into something they are not.

A point of view thus limited has of course its usefulness in practical affairs; it is neither illegitimate nor false, provided that its limitations are recognized. It is only when it begins to occupy a place that does not belong to it, and so to distract attention from other and superior points of view, that its limitations become dangerous. When it attains to a superiority over all other points of view its inherent limitation becomes disastrous, because it is then looked to as the arbiter of judgment and the source of truth. It is expected to answer questions which it is not qualified to answer and to solve problems which it should never have been asked to solve. Having reached that point it finds itself compelled to seek to explain the observed phenomenon of Religion in terms of its own outlook. Its philosophical and psychological departments are brought into play; they have made a close and detailed study of Religion in all its observable aspects, and since the esoteric domain is not without its outward manifestations, it is not excluded. Hence many books and lectures on the nature of spiritual (or mystical) experience, which, however erudite they may be, can only circle round and round their objective without ever getting nearer to it. Any result they may arrive at can only be a product of imagination. Hence also many attempts to find a psychological explanation of the religious phenomenon and of the idea of God. Such attempts have sometimes led to the attribution of a quasi-divine status to some kind of collective psychic tendency, as if God were no more than a sum or resultant of human feelings and desires. Results of that order are the inevitable outcome of the approach. In any case, and whatever its results may be, the approach in question implies the assumption of a position of superiority over the object of its investigations—in this case Religion. To attempt to explain or to account for Religion in modern scientific terms is simply an attempt to account for the greater in terms of the less, which is impossible. The very principle and purpose of modern science is to leave no room for the incomparable, thus excluding all that is greater than itself.

Metaphysical science has already been mentioned. Its very name, which can accurately be said to mean beyond the observable, indicates that it is wholly outside the purview of modern science. It is no doubt for this reason that it is nowadays either ignored or set aside as vague and inexact or as having little relation to real life, or as not being really scientific. It is indeed impossible from the modern scientific point of view to see what it is about. It is nevertheless a science of extreme precision and supreme relevance. To say that it is the science of the Infinite or the science of Reality does not help very much, though it is true. The reader will however see that if so it cannot be unrelated to the subject of Chapter 3.

To say that metaphysical science is the science of Divinity would be—or would appear to be—unduly specific. Its human foundation is not observation but vision, direct, intuitive and non-analytical, having as its object that which underlies the relative reality of all things and is the principle of existence. Such vision is sufficient to itself and needs no exposition, but few indeed are those to whom it has been granted in its fullness.

In those to whom it has been granted in any degree it is usually very partial. Among them there are some whose approach is naturally intellectual (though not in any narrow sense of the word). It is for these last that metaphysical science in its expository form exists. As being among those who are beyond question its greatest exponents one could name Chuang Tzu, Shankara, Plotinus, Ibn 'Arabī, and Meister Eckhart. It is both implicit and explicit in the Sacred Scriptures of all Traditions and in the writings of their orthodox commentators. It differs from modern science in that it always leaves room for the inexpressible, and for that reason its outward expression can take many different forms. The appreciation of those forms depends on the degree and kind of vision that accompanies their study. Where vision is lacking their true import can never be grasped.

From the point of view of modern science and philosophy alone—and the former includes psychology in all its branches—it is not possible to see what Tradition stands for, nor what Religion is. It is in contrast possible in the light of Tradition and of metaphysical science to see what modern science is and what it stands for. Its very foundation and principle is agnostic.[3]

Closely related to the observational character of modern science is its rationalistic character. The combination of accurate observation and logical reasoning is held to be, if not infallible, at least potentially all-sufficient. This is a case of exalting something above its proper status. Reason is indeed a wonderful gift, of great power and usefulness; but none the less it is a tool and no more. As such it can be used well or badly. However good a tool may be, and however skillfully it is used, it cannot produce sound work from inadequate material. Reason likewise must have good material in the form of

---

3. Atheism is hot, stupid and obstinate; agnosticism is the same thing in a cold, clever and pretentious form. Are not these three epithets curiously apposite in relation to modern science?

data to work on; one cannot reason about nothing, nor usefully about trivialities, nor can one produce valid conclusions from inadequate data. It is a waste of time to develop and elaborate the reasoning faculty if the real trouble is the incompleteness of the material at its disposal, that is to say, a lack of vision. We come back to the point that the restriction of the field of vision of modern science is the key to the situation. It has been said that 'where there is no vision, the people perish',[4] and one might venture to add 'however well-developed their reasoning powers'. It has also been said that the Kingdom of God 'cometh not with observation'.[5]

Besides being rationalistic, modern science is strongly humanistic. It envisages man not only as the seer, the planner and the doer, but also as the sole beneficiary of his own activities. The service of mankind being its first and only objective, it places mankind in the position of that to which all service is due.[6]

Someone will doubtless say: 'I agree so far as the obvious superfluities of modern civilization are concerned, but what about the no less obviously real benefits, for instance those realized in the field of medicine and public health? Surely the enormous advances made in surgery, in anesthetics and in the treatment of disease in general, including the virtual elimination of certain scourges like bubonic plague and typhus, together with many evident improvements made in other fields—surely all these things count for something'!

Any fully valid criterion must take into account the salvation of souls. So far as that is concerned, the advantages claimed are, in principle, neutral. Their effect may be good or bad or none. Their evident advantages from a terrestrial point of view are the main items on the credit side of the account of modern science—or of its product, modern civilization. It is a mistake however to look at one side of an account and not the other, since both are parts of a picture

---

4. Prov. 29:18.
5. Luke 17:20.
6. Somebody in Russia announced not long ago that 'the people are now God', and in a certain sense he was not far wrong. Since any such idea represents a complete inversion of the inescapable, providential and factual situation of mankind, it is about as totally unrealistic as anything could be, and cannot therefore reasonably be expected to do any good to mankind or to anything else.

of the same thing. In this case the main item on the debit side is the thrusting into the background, obscuration and final perversion of the means of grace that alone can make life worth living at all. Through grace alone is life sanctified and made acceptable to the God who gave it, and to whom it must be returned. If that be so, the price paid for these advantages is incommensurably too high.

Even the credit side of the account is however not as strong as some people would make it out to be. In the realm of applied science, where modern science and industry go hand in hand, the revolution brought about by the flood of innovations cannot be expected to lead to a better state of affairs unless successive and, in principle, unlimited additions of facilities, comforts and services, are as beneficial in all circumstances as they are assumed to be. So far, the expected benefits from the already great progress achieved do not appear to have been realized. People are neither better, happier nor more secure than they used to be; some would say that they are less so. This may be because, as is often argued, we do not yet know how to use the new possibilities opened up, so we divert them, for instance, to preparations for war; or it may be because the speed of change has been too great, so that civilization is subject to growing pains. But both preparations for war and the speed of change are accelerating almost daily, so that there seems to be no hope of catching up.[7]

The common proposition, to the effect that what is needed is more science, more research, and therefore inevitably more possibilities liable to misuse and an even greater speed of change, seems difficult to sustain logically. It appears in fact that the solution of each problem raises further problems more quickly than they can be dealt with. More and more research and more and more urgent action seem always to be called for. It appears also that the recent widespread increase in wealth, services and facilities has produced an insatiability which neutralizes the contentment they are expected to bring. Yet that kind of insatiability seems to be a condition of the prosperity of industry.

---

7. One might almost as well admit at once that, whatever has the last word, it is not modern science, and that there is something else more powerful than it.

There is of course a short answer to all this. The Traditions are unanimous in teaching that wealth and comforts are not in themselves bad, but that they become so if pursued either to excess or for their own sakes. Then they become idols. The soul becomes attached to them and not to God. The pursuit of the lesser good becomes a distraction from the pursuit of the greater good.

At death the soul is parted from its worldly possessions, and if it has not, so to speak, prepared a home for itself elsewhere, it is lost. Let it not be forgotten that worldly possessions include all erudition, all discursive knowledge and the whole of modern science and its terrestrial results. All must die, and nothing will be left but vision; a vision, however, so sharpened that the soul will see the true value of all that it has possessed and all that it has missed, and will come to 'know as it is known'. The observer will at last 'know himself' and thereby what it really was that he was observing. Sensorial perception, discursive thought and reason itself are of the things that perish with the body. Like the body, they are at the same time instruments of action and veils temporarily obscuring the vision that alone endures.

If the attainment of predominance by the point of view of which modern science is the most typical product represents an emergence from darkness into light—as is so frequently asserted and widely believed—we have only to pursue the way we have chosen and all will be well, if not for us, at least for our descendants. But if, as Tradition maintains, the hereafter (or whatever you choose to call it) is immeasurably more real and more enduring than the life of this world, and if the whole-hearted pursuit of the latter excludes the whole-hearted pursuit of the former, the inescapable conclusion is that the way we have chosen is not an emergence from darkness into light, but on the contrary the abandonment of a light, dimly though it may have been seen, and a plunge into obscurity and confusion.

Many people find it difficult or impossible to accept any such view. If they could the situation would not be what it is. Those for whom it is the only acceptable view, because it is the only one that makes the contemporary scene intelligible, should beware of blaming the scientists and excusing themselves. For it is we, the nonspecialists, who have allowed ourselves to be deluded into thinking that we control our own ultimate destiny or that of our children. Neither history nor experience appears to have any effect in removing that delusion. We have allowed ourselves to be deluded into thinking that we are achieving, or could achieve, or would benefit if we could achieve, a conquest of Nature whereby the whole nonhuman world is enslaved to us and ministers to our desires. It does not seem to occur to us, even to those of us who profess a belief in God, that any such notion is not only ludicrously presumptuous, but also, since the world belongs to God and not to us, positively blasphemous. We forget, too, that man is his own worst enemy. It is his own proud and greedy nature that needs to be conquered, and not a nature conceived as something outside himself and turned, by his own imagination alone, into an enemy.

Meanwhile this illusory conquest of nature is commonly supposed to be in course of achievement. The real satisfactions it should bring seem to be always round the corner. Life can seldom before have been so hurried, confused and obsessed by fears and antagonisms and mutual incomprehension.

There is a Bible story particularly apposite to this situation. The inhabitants of Babel tried to reach heaven by building an enormous tower. The tower was entirely a product of their own ingenuity and efforts, and the heaven it was designed to reach was illusory (since however high they had built they would not have found anything). The result was rather unexpected: it was an inextricable confusion arising from the fact that they ceased to be able to understand one another.

6

ART ANCIENT
& MODERN

IT has been truly said that 'art is the mirror of its times.' This implies that the peculiarities characteristic of a given period are reflected in the art of that period. But this is only half the truth, because art not only reflects its times: it also exercises a powerful influence over them.

A work of art is distinguished from other products of human skill by the fact that it is, to a greater or less extent, inspired. This inspiration confers upon it a value or a significance which it would otherwise lack.

Inspiration can be of different kinds and can come from various sources. The difference between a work of art that is ancient in spirit and one that is modern in spirit resides fundamentally in a difference in the nature of its inspiration and in the source from which that inspiration comes. Neither category can be established by date alone, but art that is ancient in spirit predominates in ancient times, and *vice versa*.

Broadly speaking, the distinction can be expressed in the following way. The artist whose work is ancient in spirit, whatever he may take as his model, derives his inspiration from Tradition. This is perhaps most evident when the art in question is specifically religious in character, and when the artist prepares himself for work by prayer, fasting and meditation, as would be normal for the painting of an icon or a Tibetan *tan'ka*, or in preparation for a religious drama. In such cases the artist can be said to seek his inspiration directly from God, though in addition he is always guided, usually very closely, by traditional rules governing his method, style and choice of model. If his art is not specifically religious in character, as is the case if he is a craftsman producing articles of daily use, he is similarly guided by Tradition in his method, style and choice of model. Although his inspiration is then in a sense less direct than in the first case, nevertheless it comes from the same source and is no less real. In both cases the artist is indeed constrained by Tradition. He must not allow free play to his imagination and he must not experiment beyond a certain clearly defined point. This constraint protects him from error, from his own individual weakness in the face of subversive influences and from isolation. The last thing he would wish, if the possibility ever occurred to him, would be to be released from it.

Judging by the admiration that is so justly and universally accorded to them, it certainly cannot be said that works of art that are ancient in spirit bear the marks of a constraint that has impaired their quality or their beauty. If that constraint is, artistically speaking, otherwise than beneficial, how is it that so many common traditional objects—a cottage, a cornstack, a wagon, a scythe, a basket, for example—are so evidently works of art, and at the same time show great variety of form, even within a single country, whereas the corresponding modern objects—a concrete dwelling, a grain silo, a tractor trailer, a mowing machine, a plastic container—are not only often ugly but also increasingly alike all over the world?

The artist whose work is modern in spirit derives his inspiration from his environment rather than from Tradition. His environment includes not only the whole of the external world in its endless variety, but also the content of his own imagination. His mind is incapable of forming images that are not derived from his environment, however convinced he may be that they originate in himself.

The environment has always provided art with its models, but not always with its inspiration. Herein resides the fundamental distinction. In Europe the Renaissance marks the period at which the change from one source of inspiration to the other became, rather suddenly, almost complete.

The artist inspired by Tradition looks upon his model primarily as a symbol manifesting particular Divine qualities or attributes, and he seeks to embody them in his work, even though very often he would not or could not define his aim in precisely that way. Insofar as he succeeds the work will reflect, more or less directly and positively, some aspect of Ultimate Reality. It will manifest, to a greater or less degree, a supra-individual quality, a celestial as well as a terrestrial beauty. The intrinsic characteristics of the model, that is to say, the peculiarities which distinguish it when it is regarded as an independent object, are a secondary consideration, and are often conventionalized, in the sense of being modified so as to conform to a traditional style.

The non-Traditional artist who looks to his environment, or to some part of it, for example to his model itself, for inspiration sees his model only as an independent object having particular intrinsic characteristics which he seeks to reproduce in his work. Since he can only reproduce characteristics that are perceptible to him as an individual, his work will itself be individual, that is to say, confined to the plane on which his individuality is manifested; it will not manifest the quality of universality characteristic of traditional art. This is true even though the artist is completely successful in realizing his aim, and even though the qualities reproduced in his work are all desirable and good—such as beauty, strength, tenderness and so on. The work will not reflect directly and positively some aspect of Ultimate Reality. Yet since there is nothing that does not reflect that Reality, however indirectly, either positively or negatively, it will not be protected by the constraint of Tradition from a tendency towards inversion or negation. The modern artist is indeed free: free from the constraint of Tradition, and so cut off from its protection. His own judgment is the final arbiter of everything he does. In his isolation and loneliness he has no sure means of discrimination between one kind of influence and another, or between one kind of inspiration and another.

Every worker, and not the artist alone, finds himself in a comparable situation when there has been a departure from the traditional laws and constraints that alone can confer on a civilization as a whole an effective unity, so that all its constituent parts—Religion, art, politics, trade, sport—are as one. When the principle of unity has been lost to sight everything becomes individualized. Chaos can only be avoided by some kind of collectivization of human society, in an attempt to reconstruct the missing unity. But any such collectivization is but superficial and lacks a sure foundation. It inevitably takes the form of a grouping together of like with like, rather than a hierarchical organization of like with unlike, such as exists in a traditional civilization. Without a hierarchical organization, a civilization is broken up in the course of its history into a growing number of separate domains, each one representing a particular set of objectives and points of view, for example, Religion, politics, economics, science, art, industry, trade, sport and so on. They are more or less loosely interconnected by such interests as they have in common, but each claims a certain independence and often a certain supremacy, while at the same time each tends to split up into a number of subsidiary domains.

Thus it is that the artistic or 'cultural' domain, with which we are here concerned, comes into being as a more or less distinct entity. Its separate existence is a relatively recent phenomenon. For a long time past the arts have played a less and less real and effective part in the life of the community, on which they are now to a large extent superimposed as a luxury or a compensation. In our society the supremacy of modern science and its related domains of industry and economics are in practice unquestioned. Beauty being the quality most particularly sought after in the arts—at least hitherto—a consequence of this separation of domains has been a divorce of beauty from utility. The useful often becomes ugly and the beautiful useless.[1] Beauty ceases to be a quality occurring naturally in the products of human skill; instead, it has to be added artificially or artistically. This tends to happen only when it does not interfere unduly with the economics of production, or when it can be turned into an economic asset and used to promote consumer acceptance.

Thus, while applied art has a connection, purely exterior and economic, with some of the other factors that make up the life of the

---

1. Beauty becomes a superfluity, a luxury to be cultivated for its own sake, or to be grafted in the form of applied art (the notion of which would have been incomprehensible in an earlier age) on to the ugliness that is the characteristic of a profane civilization.

community, fine art forms a domain of its own within which it becomes increasingly isolated. In this abnormal situation art can only seek its justification within itself; and since the attention of the artist, no less than that of his public, is henceforth directed to his experience of his environment, that is to say, to the experience of the senses, that justification can only be aesthetic, that is to say, concerned with the gratification of the senses.

In the earlier stages of this movement a sufficient aesthetic satisfaction, and with it a certain justification of art, is obtained through the simple representation of the beauties of nature. The recording and aesthetic interpretation of natural beauty becomes the main aim and function of art. It demands a high degree of perceptiveness, discrimination and skill, and when it is successful its products can be very beautiful. Nothing that is in any way beautiful is wholly despicable or worthless. Nevertheless, such work is no longer traditional in the rightful sense of the word. The source of its inspiration is not Tradition but the environment. However true to life it may be, it is no longer true to the real nature and destiny of man. However much satisfaction it may give, it takes no account of, and contributes nothing to, the fulfillment of that destiny.

Someone will say: 'But surely, even if that be true of profane art, it cannot be true of religious art.' Unfortunately it can indeed be true of religious art, particularly if, as is usually the case, the words 'religious art' signify no more than an art that takes a religious subject as its model. The criterion of the traditional character of a work is not one of date nor of model: it is one of inspiration and style.

The essential reason why the representation of natural beauty cannot by itself be fully satisfying is that it does not satisfy the fundamental need, unconscious though it often be, for something greater and more enduring than terrestrial experience. It caters in general for a need that is occasional and contingent, and subject to the fluctuations of individual taste and opinion, and even of fashion. Hence the quest for something that will be more fully satisfying, or, in default of satisfaction, that will at least attract attention, puzzle or horrify. The quest is for novelty and originality at all costs. This is the exact equivalent of the sensationalism so evident in some other domains. The artist, if he is to survive, is virtually compelled to explore his environment (which, be it remembered, includes the content of his imagination) to its uttermost limits in a search for fresh models and fresh sources of inspiration. Having as it were exhausted the resources of those parts of his environment that affect his senses from without, he must probe into that part that affects his sensibilities from within. The regions he explores contain a vast and amorphous array of psychic entities and influences, some derived from his own subconscious mind, others from some kind of collective psychic influence, and others from the psychic world as such. Modern psychology tries to describe and to classify the few elements of this array that are accessible to analysis, and gives them high-sounding scientific names.

In the old days they were called good or bad fairies or spirits, or demons or ghosts or bogeys, and by many other names. It was certainly then recognized that Tradition alone, whether religious in form or otherwise, could be relied on to keep them in order, to favor the good influences and suppress the bad.[2]

In the absence of the control which Tradition alone can exercise, it is extremely dangerous to venture into the territory of these powerful, ill-defined and deceptive psychic forces. It is, however, characteristic of the later phases of an historical cycle that all its most subversive and dissolving elements, hitherto kept in the darkness where they normally belong, should be brought into the light of day. Modern psychology has no idea how to set about the destruction of these elements (our ancestors would have said: 'how to exorcise them'), nor does it recognize the fact that such things cannot be brought into the light of day otherwise than by their taking possession of some of the elements that make up a human society, which then acts as their vehicle; or in other words, without the occurrence

---

2. Such was the purpose of many of the traditional sciences that are now virtually obsolete and usually dismissed as mere magic or superstition, as if our ancestors were so idiotic as to be incapable of distinguishing illusory results from real ones, or good from bad. On the contrary, it is the supposed ineffectuality of those sciences that is a delusion, and a dangerous one. Their subsisting residues have become superstitions in the proper sense of the word, namely, ancient forms detached from their origin and no longer comprehended. They are not for that reason deprived of their power, which however is no longer under control.

of changes in a human society favorable to the development of their influence, so that a point is eventually reached where their destruction cannot be accomplished without the destruction of the society itself.

A similar failure to recognize the nature of the forces in question accompanies the activities of those artists who deliberately lay themselves open to the influence of psychic forces in an attempt to widen the field from which they draw their inspiration. Small wonder that the result so often seems 'satanic' to anyone who has eyes to see or ears to hear, and who is not misled by current mumbo-jumbo about 'creative art', 'significant form' and so on. The incomprehensibility of much modern art has produced a whole new jargon of apologetics, miscalled criticism, without which that art could not survive the ponderous and unanalytical conservatism of the masses. This conservatism, on the whole negative in character, is not for that reason anti-traditional in tendency. It is in this sense that *vox populi* can also be *vox Dei*.

Let it be clearly understood that no man ever created anything whatsoever; not a speck of dust, not even an idea, for all ideas are derived from pre-existing material. The most that man can do, and that only to a very limited extent, is to select and arrange what is already there.

Significance as such in no way justifies anything, the crux of the matter being what it is that is signified. Forms, and not least the forms of art, can have a significance that is sacred and unitive, or one that is diabolical and disruptive. The latter are often deceptive, for the sacred is profound with the profundity and mystery of the star-spangled heavens, while the diabolical is also profound, but in the opposite sense, with the hot and heavy obscurity of the nether regions. An unguided soul can all too easily mistake the one profundity for the other. The sacred is interior in the sense that it is associated with the spiritual Centre that is everywhere; the diabolical is interior in the sense that it is associated with the centre of gravity towards which all material things tend.

We are contrasting an inspiration arising from Tradition with an inspiration (which ought really to be called a pseudo-inspiration) sought in appearances. This last leads inevitably to a search for a missing inwardness. The artist feels compelled to seek it; very often he finds nothing, but if he finds anything it is almost certainly not a spiritual inwardness, but rather physical or psychic.

The validity of a work of art is often assessed on the grounds of the sincerity of the artist. The implication presumably is that he is not trying to deceive or to defraud anyone, but is on the contrary convinced that his approach to his work is valid, and that therefore, provided that he does his work well, its results must be good. This notion is closely related to another, not at all uncommon nowadays, to the effect that whatever one believes to be right is for that reason right. Both notions are equally vicious and equally absurd. They are not so much a contradiction of truth as a denial that there is any such thing as truth.

Curiously enough, the same principle does not seem to be applied to most other domains, such as those of politics or economics or modern science, where it would be generally admitted that a man can be disastrously wrong, however convinced he may be that he is right. This is probably because the things included in the other domains named are regarded as being more or less measurable, whereas those included in the aesthetic domain are too subtle and difficult to define or measure. They are therefore relegated to a region wherein individual opinion and taste are supreme. If that be so, it becomes understandable that the same criteria should be applied to the ultimate or metaphysical truth—or to Religion, its most direct expression—since its domain (if this word be still applicable) is so comprehensive as to include all domains, and is accordingly immeasurable.

The change of approach described and its consequential developments can be discerned in all the arts, but perhaps most easily in the visual arts, painting and sculpture, where the forms chosen by the artist as his models are visible and relatively stable. The forms chosen as models in the literary arts are usually events rather than objects; but events, and thoughts as well, possess form just as do visible objects. They can similarly be taken either as symbols or as mere incidents. Anyone who questions this has only to reflect on the forms of the Sacred Scriptures, and on the substitution of a mere literal rendering for their symbolical interpretation. Architecture, with its predominantly utilitarian bias and non-representational character, reflects the changes in question perhaps most clearly when it is employed in the service of Religion: it is sufficient to compare the forms of medieval churches with those of many modernistic churches.

There remains music, the most abstract and non-representational of all the arts, and its associated art, the dance. Each would be worthy of a separate study, but only a few points can be mentioned here.

Certain kinds of modern dancing manifest the spirit of decadence at least as obviously as does any other modern art. Indeed it is open to question whether they still fall into the category of art. Apart from any question of symbolical content, their total lack of the grace and dignity of traditional dancing needs no emphasis.

As for music itself, its abstract character has generally speaking afforded it some protection against those influences to which the more representational arts are more vulnerable. Nevertheless, as in other arts, a growing preoccupation with a purely sensual beauty has led to an urge continually to try to break new ground in the hope of finding new material and new inspiration. This has led, among other things, to the borrowing of elements from the sacred music of other Traditions. For instance, the sacred rhythms of African music, which are essentially ritual in origin, acquire, when they are alienated from the Tradition to which they belong, all the subversive and deceptive characteristics of superstitions in the proper sense of the word. They lose their sacred character, but not their power, and there is nothing to hold that power in check or to direct it aright. The fact that such considerations are largely rejected by the modern outlook in no way detracts from their reality; indeed incomprehension of such matters is entirely characteristic of the modern outlook.

Although music has to a certain extent been protected by its non-representational character from some of the influences that have affected other arts, yet there is one peculiarity in its history which exemplifies with particular clarity the real nature of the changes that have taken place. In most ancient music a single note of unchanging pitch is sounded continuously throughout the composition; the melody departs from it and returns to it, often frequently, and is as it were no more than a development of possibilities inherent in the continuous note, the 'tonic', the origin, the support and the end of all the rest. Some music of this kind has survived to the present day, for example that of the bagpipes.[3] At a later stage the continuous sounding of the tonic is abandoned, but the melody is still developed in such a way that the tonic, even when unheard, is effectively present; the French *sous-entendu* conveys this exactly; the melody never changes its key or tonality.

Next comes the discovery (really the release of a possibility formerly held in check) of the sensational effect of modulation, a change of key. At first such changes were restricted to a narrow range of keys closely related to the original key, a final return to which was obligatory. Later modulation becomes a dominant element in music, now spread by mechanical reproduction all over the world. It is no longer restricted to nearly related keys, all keys being regarded as equivalent and interchangeable.[4] This involves a loss of both the stability and the subtlety of a music in which each key, usually called a mode, is qualitatively different from every other. Thus the tonic, the unchanging principial note in which traditional melody begins, develops and ends, is gradually allowed to slip into the background, and to be overwhelmed by the development of possibilities which, attractive though they be, and indeed necessary for the full manifestation of all the possibilities inherent in music as an art (and therefore also inherent in the tonic itself), are none the less negative insofar as they are incompatible with the maintenance of the audibility of the tonic; or, one might say, incompatible with its 'real presence'. A final and totally dissolving step is taken in the

3. The rules governing the development of the melody, and those governing any polyphonic or harmonic additions to it, differ according to the traditional style of the music, and do not affect the immediate point.

4. This new freedom necessitated the invention of the 'well tempered' scale, in which all keys are effectively interchangeable, because they differ only in pitch, so that there is a complete and exciting freedom of movement between any one and any other; but that freedom cannot be achieved without the sacrifice of the exceedingly fine differences of pitch which distinguish the natural scale from the well-tempered scale, the latter being indeed a more or less artificial compromise.

invention of atonal music, wherein any impression of tonality is studiously avoided, as a matter, one might say, of pseudo-principle.

These developments reflect accurately in the domain of music the successive stages of the abrogation and final abandonment in all domains of the traditional laws governing the activities taking place within those domains. The main purpose and effect of these laws was to ensure a constant reference back in each domain to the underlying principle of its existence. That principle cannot be other than the Principle of all existence; its origin, its support and its end.

The successive abrogations in all fields of art succeed one another ever more rapidly; they are, broadly speaking, all undertaken in the name of freedom. In the arts, as in other domains, each new freedom is more illusory than its predecessor, since it always consists in a substitution of other constraints for the constraints of Tradition. The new constraints, though often unrecognized as such, confine the artist ever more closely to terrestrial things, and so cut off his access to heavenly things, thus depriving him of the only freedom worth having, indeed of the only real freedom there is.

As time goes on it is inevitable that the qualities normally associated with a work of art should be sacrificed one by one on the altar of this imaginary freedom, often spoken of as 'originality'. But only a work of art that is traditional in spirit can properly be called 'original', because it alone is effectively attached to its real origin. The newer kind of originality assumes that man, not God, is the origin and the creator, and that inspiration is individual and not universal.

At last even the ideal of a purely sensual beauty is often sacrificed. It will perhaps be argued that this is not really so, but that a new kind of beauty always takes the place of one that has been abandoned, and that this new beauty is inevitably unrecognized at first and condemned as ugliness, until the public have been educated to it. There is an element of truth in this, but it is contingent on a recognition of the fact that each successive new expression of beauty derives less and less of its inspiration from heavenly things and more and more from earthly things, and from them in descending order. The public is therefore not 'educated up' but 'educated down'. It is a question of getting accustomed to things that are qualitatively inferior; it is as such that they are instinctively resisted at first, however novel and sensational they may be. Their inferiority is directly reflected in their lack of an enduring influence and in the confused quality of that influence, as well as in the perishability of their forms.

An acceptance of the inferior takes place only when there is a failure to distinguish on the one hand between a relative good, dusty and tarnished though it be, which is still not error, and on the other a polished and glittering relative error. Beauty as such is on the side of good; that it should become tarnished is a misfortune. That it should be lost is a disaster.

The saying that 'beauty is in the eye of the beholder' is scarcely as much as a half-truth. It belittles beauty by suggesting that it is less than the beholder and dependent on him, or that it is purely subjective in the psychological sense. The saying is true only in the sense that different people see different kinds of beauty, or none at all, as the case may be. It ignores the truth that beauty as a divine attribute is greater than the beholder who is but an individual. Beauty exists on all planes of manifestation: we see only its reflection on a lower plane, whereon it is a manifestation of the Infinite in the finite, a gift of God, a grace, a sign, a symbol, though its vehicle be limited and ephemeral. Fortunate indeed is the man who sees both the vehicle and the beauty it carries for what each really is.

7

WHAT AM I?

THAT which perceives is what each of us knows as 'I'. There is no perception unaccompanied by a change in the perceiver. A visible external object, for instance, initiates a complex series of changes in the eye, its nerves and the brain; but none of these organs considered together or separately can be said to see, nor do the changes they undergo constitute vision. There is something else, something that interprets the changes and deduces the qualities of the object seen not only separately as form, color texture, size, etc., but also synthetically, so that it is instantly recognized as a man or an apple or a star.

If the mechanism (eye-nerve-brain) is faulty, and equally if the faculty of interpretation is limited or lacking (as it so evidently is in varying degrees in all animals), the object is not perceived for what it is, or is not perceived at all. Similarly with the other senses. Similarly also with all deduction originating in sense-perception.

Thus there can be no awareness which is not already potentially present in the individual who is aware. What we perceive or know is what we are capable of perceiving and knowing, rather than what there is to be perceived and known. 'My' perception and 'my' knowledge comprise far more of 'me' than of the indefinite range of possibilities that constitute my environment, and *a fortiori* of the limitless possibilities of the Infinite. My knowledge is objective only to the extent that there is a real correspondence between my own nature and the nature of the universe. Hence the answer to all questions connected directly or indirectly with the nature or the reality or the objectivity of the universe or of anything within it is contingent on, or can be reduced to, the single crucial question: 'What am I?'

That question can never be fully answered by observation. I am more than anything that I can observe or feel or think about. Observation, sensation and mentation imply a duality between myself and some object that is not myself. We commonly speak of 'my' body or 'my' soul in the same way as we speak of 'my' feelings or 'my' hand or 'my' dog. I am however certainly nothing that I can be said to possess. We also commonly use phrases like 'I said to myself' or 'I am ashamed of myself.' Then who or what is the 'I' that says these things? It is not my body; it is not my soul. It cannot be the 'myself' of which 'I' am ashamed, nor can it be said to be anything in particular other than these.

If I argue that I am a man and I know what a man is, I delude myself; for I do not know what a man is unless I know what I am. If I practice introspection in the psychological sense, I am merely trying to isolate parts or qualities of my total being and to observe them objectively. The ultimate 'I', the 'pure subject', eludes all research.

Traditionally the ultimate 'I' is the Self or Personality (with initial capitals) considered as being transcendent with respect to everything distinctive—including the lesser self or personality which is the individual ego, perceptible and distinctively knowable. The transcendent Self can never be specified or objectivized, proved or disproved: yet it is the one ultimate certitude lying at the heart of the being of every one of us. To realize what that transpersonal self is is to realize 'what I am', and thereby to have at my disposal the indispensable key to all knowledge.

How, then, to find the answer to the question 'what am I?' Evidently modern science and philosophy are likely to take us farther from it rather than nearer to it, for before they could make any approach to the answer they would have to cease to be what they are. It is in the nature of the case that the answer can never be categorical; insofar as it can be expressed at all it must be expressed symbolically. Perhaps enough hints have already been given as to where the appropriate symbols may be sought.

There will be no harm in devoting a little attention to its obvious corollary: 'What is my neighbor?' From his point of view (to which I must accord an authority equal to my own) it is he who is 'I' and I whom am his neighbor. Are we then simply two creatures of the same species who naturally look at things in the same way? Or alternatively, is it that the same transcendent Self is manifested in us both, so that an essential unity is reflected in an apparent duality?

The modern scientific approach cannot get beyond the first answer; but sometimes it tries to, and then it is inevitably led into an attempt to define the Self, which, being not other than the ultimate 'I', is indefinable. The result is therefore a distortion of the truth.

The second answer is the answer of Tradition, and therefore of Religion. Since Religion must cater for the needs of all men, it has to interpret that answer in such a way that all men may understand it, not so much mentally as existentially; not so much in their brains as in their hearts, so that, whether or not they may be able to express the truth in words, they may be enabled to live according to it.

That is the essence and origin of the religious virtues, of which charity may be taken as an example. Charity is an essential component of all Religions (the Christian Religion is far from having any sort of monopoly) because, in the last analysis and in its only pure form, charity is the recognition of the fundamental identity of myself and my neighbor.

If my only certitude, the one thing it does not occur to me to question, is that I am 'I', I cannot, unless I am a solipsist, refuse to recognize that my neighbor is no less 'I' than I am. If that is the case why should I behave as if my 'I' were other or better than his? Should I not 'do unto him as I would that he should do unto me', 'love him as myself'? Instead, the tendency is always to pay attention to our apparent distinction and to the details of the relatively small differences between us. We each embody but a tiny fragment of the indefinitely extensive possibilities of our common 'being'; it is 'being' and its indefinite possibilities that are real: all the rest is but a fragmented manifestation of those possibilities in a temporal and distinctive mode. All but the underlying and non-distinctive reality of being is therefore in a very real sense illusory, a reflection that vanishes when the conditions that produced it change, and with precisely the degree of reality that attaches to a reflection. Insofar as our actions are not in conformity with reality, we blur its reflected image in the world. If we do not act charitably to our neighbor, our actions are not in conformity with the reality of our essential identity; we blur the truth so that it becomes not only less and less visible but also less and less the foundation of our living.

True charity is therefore by no means synonymous with altruism, for altruism as such tends to be more separative than unitive. It starts from the assumption, as its very name indicates, that my neighbor is other than I. Sentiment should not be the prime mover of charity, though sentiment has a part to play. Still less is the word 'charity' properly applicable to the mere act of giving something to somebody. On the contrary, its closest associations are with reality and truth, and with the finding of the answer to the question: 'What am I'?

Thus the charity that is common to all Religions is above all realistic, being founded on a true view of the nature of things. It does not always coincide with a charity motivated largely by sentiment.

A realistic charity is regulated by two overriding considerations. The first is that, since everything came from God and finds its fulfillment in a return to Him, the service of God comes before the service of man, with the corollary that the latter is useful only insofar as it is an expression of service to God.[1] In terms of Christianity the two New Testament commandments mean what they say. The normal practical expression of service to God being adherence to Tradition, that is what comes first, and the charitable act must not interfere with or contradict traditional laws, including those that preserve the equilibrium of society, either because they serve to maintain the social hierarchy, or because they provide for the punishment of the wicked.

The second consideration is that charity is not realistic if it offers a lesser good, or a false good, in place of the true good. This may happen simply because a man does not do to his neighbor as he would like his neighbor to do to him. For example, it may be that he himself would hate to be interfered with and told that he does not know what is good for him, and would be furious if someone ran a subscription to educate or to improve him; but such considerations may not prevent him from doing exactly those things to his neighbour. Owing to his ignorance of what he is and what his neighbor is,

1. See Deut. 6:4–7.

he may really not know what is good for either. A man may in all good faith offer to his neighbor something that will distract the latter from what he really needs most—thus offering him a stone in place of bread, or a serpent in place of a fish.[2] No man can give what he does not possess; and that is why to 'covet earnestly the best gifts'[3] is the beginning of charity. The passing on of those gifts, once possessed, will look after itself.

Charity is chosen as an example because it is the virtue most evidently related to the question: 'What am I' besides being the cardinal virtue of Christianity. All the other traditional virtues are similarly expressions of a conformity to reality and to truth. They are by no means merely useful conventions or expedients devised to minimize conflict, external or internal, or to make life more agreeable. Therefore, when truth flies out of the window, true virtue soon follows.

It is not their outward forms that make the virtues effective, either for the salvation of the soul or for anything else. What makes them effective in any particular case is their animation by an inward consciousness of, or conformity to, the real nature of the cosmos. It is he who gives 'a cup of water' (the most insignificant of charitable acts) 'in my name' who will 'not lose his reward'.[4] The same act performed in any other name, for example in the name of humanity, retains all its natural insignificance and may not even escape from perversion to diabolical ends.

Consciousness of reality can take the form of a metaphysical realization of what I am, implying a simultaneous realization of what my neighbor is. Conformity to reality can find its expression in religious faith, with all that this implies by way of participation in the doctrinal, ritual and ethical elements of Religion. There is no rigid line of demarcation between consciousness and conformity, but the attainment of the former otherwise than by way of the latter is so rare that it can be left out of account as a practical possibility.

The one thing that can be stated categorically is that a true consciousness of reality can never be attained by observation.

2. Matt. 7:9–10.
3. 1 Cor. 12:31.
4. Mark 9:41.

8

DECADENCE
& IDOLATRY

THE word decadence means falling off or falling away. The contemporary decadence of Religion, the existence of which few would dispute, is something very much more than a mere reduction in the number of its adherents or in the influence it exercises.

Decadence is not the same thing as either deviation or perversion. Decadence is an enfeeblement, deviation is a going astray and perversion is a reversal of intent. Or it could be said that decadence is a loss of power, deviation a waste of power and perversion an abuse of power. Nevertheless decadence, deviation and perversion overlap and merge one into another. If decadence is here treated separately it is only in order to avoid a descriptive confusion as great as that prevailing in the situation described. That situation is highly unstable and constantly changing. All that can be attempted is a background sketch into which details can be fitted as they arise.

Anyone who understands what Tradition is will also understand that a falling away from the primordial purity and perfection of a new Revelation is inevitable as time goes on. He will understand too that it is not the spirit of Religion that becomes decadent or even dies, it is only its temporary embodiment in a human society. The vital spark is inextinguishable and must be present in the world for so long as the world endures. At certain times the spark is more closely hidden than at others; and just such a time is the present.

Although the spark may be hard to locate it is not at all difficult to specify the nature of some of the clouds that hide it. They do so by distracting attention from it or by distorting the rays it emits.

The profane point of view, as its influence spreads, gradually creates a new domain for itself, composed of elements extracted from the pre-existent traditional domain together with new elements derived from itself. It is this relatively new domain which people usually have in view when they speak of 'ordinary life' or 'everyday life' or 'real life'. The domain ruled by Tradition becomes correspondingly restricted to its more specifically religious aspect, which gradually becomes virtually the only effective guardian of the vital spark. It does so only for so long, of course, as it retains its orthodoxy. On this last aspect of the question there will be more to say later on. Meanwhile 'ordinary' life continues to claim an ever-growing share of most people's attention.

The progressive restriction of the domain of Tradition and Religion is brought about in part by annexation and in part by the introduction of new distractions, most of them apparently in themselves harmless, and nearly always presented as new benefits. Industrialism was hailed on its advent as the dawn of a new era of prosperity; it has now annexed almost every productive activity and every traditional craft, including agriculture, thereby subordinating the true good of humanity to the work of its own proliferation. In the process it has annexed, profaned and commercialized the holy day, together with the sports, dancing and music normally associated with it. Even the annexation of the intellectual field has been passed off as an advance: this position has been very effectively consolidated by the annexation of virtually the whole field of education.

A further consolidation has been effected through the development of distractions which, especially when made to appear new and exciting, absorb attention which might otherwise be directed to things less ephemeral, while providing a momentary compensation for the destruction of all that really makes life worth living. Not all these distractions are equally crude and obvious. Among those that are less so may be cited the enormous growth of clubs and societies, harmless and well-meaning in themselves, which tend to give their growing number of members a certain sense of unity and of belonging to something. This can act as a substitute for the far deeper sense of unity inherent in attachment to a common Tradition, and can cause the latter to be undervalued or forgotten.

More obviously distracting is the flood of reading matter, wherein if anything good appears it is immediately overwhelmed by the next wave. The question of merit scarcely counts in comparison to the effectiveness of sheer weight and insistence.

Still more obviously distracting is the gigantic overgrowth of public entertainment, culminating in television, the most pervasive and seductive of all distractions, not least to the young. It invades the very homes of the people, so that they no longer live in those homes centred on the once sacred hearth (symbol of the spark that animates all things), however simply yet realistically, but in a hallucinatory and hypnotic world divorced from all reality, even the relative reality of ordinary life. There is no need to multiply examples: the broad and evident fact is that nobody nowadays has time for Religion. There is too much else that must not be missed.

In all this hurly-burly it would be very surprising if religious faith, doctrine and practice remained unscathed. The impact of the notion of progress produces the idea that Religion needs to be brought up to date. This can mean only one thing, namely that it must be made more worldly, more humanistic, more democratic, and that it must be made to conform to what may be called for the sake of brevity the standards of truth set by modern science and philosophy; and finally that the element of mystery (in the true sense of the word) must be reduced to a minimum or eliminated.

Now the element in Religion that can most easily be made to appear to conform to the above conditions is the third, the ethical or moral, though this conformity can never be more than a deceptive appearance. It is very difficult to force either doctrine, whether its expression be exegetic or dogmatic, or orthodox ritual to conform to the requirements of a modern progressive ideology; it is much simpler just to let them slip into the background. Hence the very notion of Religion becomes progressively reduced in scope, not only among those who are hostile or indifferent to it, but also among its adherents, by the suppression of doctrine and ritual and the over-emphasis of its ethical aspect. This last in its turn tends to assume a more and more humanistic, almost a sociological form, till all too often it becomes little more than a kind of idealism based on the hope of a triumph of virtue over vice, whereby the world is to become an easier and pleasanter place to live in.

In the end the promotion of the physical and psychic welfare of mankind comes to be identified with the establishment of the Kingdom of Heaven. In current usage, idealism is contrasted with realism, and Religion tends to be relegated to the former, and so by implication to a domain of relative unreality. An idealism of this kind is a mere utopianism; and the opponents of Religion do not miss the opportunity of making Religion out to be a utopianism based on superstition, whereas they claim that their own utopianism is practical or scientific.

Unfortunately we do in fact often see Religion (or something that passes for such) and scientific humanism competing in the same field as purveyors of social welfare. But good will is not enough: indeed it is by no means a prerogative of Religion, and still less of the Christian Religion alone.[1] Morality is not enough, and its insufficiency is one of the reasons why virtue, and the Religion with which it is increasingly identified, tends to take on an appearance of dullness. When virtue is put into practice in the name of humanity and not in the name of God it loses its *raison d'être*, as we have seen in Chapter 7.

The conception of virtue has itself become sentimentalized and softened, to the detriment of the more forceful and combative virtues, like fortitude, indifference to death, fervor, watchfulness and nobility, and most of all in the substitution of a vague and feeble tolerance for an active opposition to worldliness. Pathetic attempts are sometimes made to make out that Religion is exciting, even as exciting as a television show; but when the notions that animate it have become more or less equated with moralism, and a rather feeble moralism at that, it certainly is nothing of the kind. Hence the common idea that Religion is a killjoy, and that to be religious is to be sanctimonious and dull.

That might not matter so much if the idea were not extended to include sanctity. A saint is often thought to be no more than someone who is uncomfortably virtuous. A saint is indeed virtuous, because he is a saint; but he is not a saint because he is virtuous. No

---

1. It is impossible not to wonder how it has come about that a certain sentence in the original Greek has come to be so often translated 'On earth peace, good will to men' when what it means is 'Peace on earth to men of right intent.'

amount of virtue is by itself a qualification for sainthood. That qualification is of a different order, and may even, when founded on *gnosis*, lie on a plane where the antithesis of good and bad has already been surpassed. The world depends on its saints, for it is they who keep it in touch with God, independently of whether or not anyone is aware of their presence or of their sainthood. It is not the scientist, not the *entrepreneur*, not yet the altruist who is the real benefactor of humanity, but the saint.

The scientific approach to Religion necessarily involves treating it as no more than a particular phenomenon among other phenomena. Looked at in this way it appears as one of the aspects of the psychological make-up of humanity. It is seen as something that exists only in order to fulfil a need inherent in human nature—a need comparable in kind to the need for sleep or food or recreation.

This is a subtle misrepresentation because it is a half-truth. It conceals the fact that sleeping and eating and recreation do not constitute the justification of human existence, whereas Religion does. To try to explain everything by attributing it to human nature is merely begging the question, and is therefore only pseudo-scientific; but such explanations are often made and widely accepted, though all they do is to eliminate everything that could raise human nature above itself.

Not unrelated to this, and no less destructive, is the notion that there are two domains in human nature, one that of the intelligence and the other that of feeling, and that modern science represents the first, while Religion is concerned only with the second. As regards the first half of this proposition, enough has already been said; as regards the second, the more decadent forms of Religion undeniably give it a certain plausibility. Religion, however, is either founded on truth, in which case it is also founded on intelligence (insofar as that word has any useful meaning), or it is not, in which case it is nothing.

At this point decadence and perversion become less and less easy to distinguish. The existence of a very real decadence makes it more and more easy for the enemies of Religion to misrepresent it, and even for those who are not its enemies to become increasingly blind to its real nature. For instance, there is a very prevalent idea to the effect that some at least of the more obvious oppositions and confusions of the present day can be attributed to the fact that the world has not yet got rid of the differences which exist and always have existed between the various Religions and Traditions. In this way it is possible to make Religion a scapegoat for troubles arising from a very different cause. This leads to the suggestion that it must be, if not abolished as soon as possible, at least reformed, purified or universalized, which inevitably implies the elimination of most of its essentials; its reduction to some kind of moralism with which, it is assumed, all men could be persuaded to agree. This tendency is closely related to the desire, referred to in Chapter 9, to get rid of the institutional forms of Religion.[2]

The Sacred Scriptures have not escaped the scrutiny demanded by contemporary intellectualism. It is not the Scriptures that are harmed by this process, but only the scrutineers themselves and those who pay heed to them. If the Scriptures are indeed the Word of God and not merely the words of men, they are independent of the limitations of the mind of man, and cannot be harmed by its criticism, whether or not the latter be called higher. The purpose of the Scriptures will not be discernible to anyone who approaches them in that spirit, and his findings can only be misleading.

The purpose of the Scriptures is not to convey information, nor yet to exercise verbal persuasion, nor yet even to be understood in any restricted or purely mental sense. Their purpose is to reveal, or to support the revelation of, the incommunicable secrets of Infinity to those whose whole being (and not mind alone) is so constituted as to vibrate in unison with them. The orthodox commentaries and traditional interpretations are providential aids to this end.

When orthodox commentaries and traditional interpretations are thrust aside in favor of critical assessments, most people, even if not led astray by the critics, are left with no alternative but to make

---

2. Another instance is the liberal individualism that permeates certain sects or branches of several Religions. It is essentially anti-traditional and, although perversion may be too strong a word for it, yet it paves the way to perversion, and may merge with it in the end.

what they can of the most obvious and literal meaning of the words of the Scriptures. That meaning is always valid, but it constitutes but a fragment of the whole, and one that is all too easily misinterpreted or distorted when it is isolated and exposed to the play of individual opinion, or to the subtle attacks of more diabolical forces.

The Sacred Scriptures are integral parts of the Traditions to which they belong, and are only fully comprehensible in the light of their respective Traditions. Every Tradition provides safeguards against their misinterpretation. In Christianity in the past only the clergy had the right to expound the Scriptures; indeed for a long time it was only the clergy who knew the language in which they were written. The situation is—or was—similar in Judaism; it is effectively similar wherever literacy is not the only measure of intelligence. In Hinduism only a Brahman may study the Vedas.

This generation, hating all that is superior to itself, wants to drag down to its own level everything that could help it if only it would humble itself and recognize its own desperate need of help. It prefers to pick out from the Sacred Scriptures such parts as can be made to appear to support its own dreary sentimental moralism and utopianism, and to ignore the rest.[3]

The softening of the significance of the Sacred Scriptures affects both their outward meaning, accessible to all, and their interpretation through contemporary representatives of the traditional hierarchies. One of its most important aspects is that which concerns the punishment of the wicked, and particularly those who set up idols in place of God. Yet there is no Sacred Scripture that is not emphatic and decisive on this point, whatever may be the symbolism in which

---

3. This is no empty accusation, particularly so far as Christians are concerned, for there is no Scripture that is outwardly more severe or more demanding than the Gospels: 'Ye generation of vipers, how can ye escape the damnation of hell?' (addressed to highly respectable and respected citizens); 'If thy right hand offend thee, cut it off'; 'Sell that thou hast, and give to the poor'; 'Blessed are ye, when men shall revile you and persecute you'; and so on. These four quotations are respectively from Matt. 23:33, 5:30, 19:21, and 5:11. The following are no less relevant: Matt. 5:20, 39, and 48; 7:21–3; 8:12; 10:34–7; 12:36; 19:24; 22:14; 24:2:24; Luke 14:26–33.

it is clothed. In Christianity this aspect seems to have become particularly associated with the Old Testament, which is perhaps one reason why the Old Testament is now so largely set aside, as if it were no more than a sketchy history of a primitive people who worshipped a rather violent tribal god. If it were not in reality something very different indeed it would not stand at the heart of one of the world's great civilizations, nor would it be among the canonical books of Christianity.

The scriptural condemnations of those who worship idols are related to a much more comprehensive and widespread set of circumstances than many people suppose. Anything that is worshipped in place of God is an idol, whether it is given some material representation such as a statue or picture, or whether it exists only in the form of an ideal.[4] Whatever a man regards as the ultimate end and justification of his life, and as embodying the fulfillment of his desires, is the thing he worships, whether or not he renders lip service to anything else. If this view of the real nature of idolatry is correct, it becomes evident that the profane point of view is not only in principle agnostic, but also in principle idolatrous, and that in the highest possible degree.

Man, alone among all creatures, embodies the possibility of a conscious and voluntary affirmation of God (to his own infinite advantage). This inevitably implies that he also embodies the complementary possibility—that of a denial of God (to his own infinite detriment). From a human point of view there is no possibility of merit in the absence of a possibility of demerit. From a metaphysical point of view both possibilities have their appropriate degree of reality. Thus it is impossible, not only that there should be no idolatry in the world, but also that it should not be developed up to the limit of its potentialities. It is equally impossible that idolaters should not reap the reward of their idolatry, and they must do so, unless they repent in time, that is to say, in this life while they are still free to do so.

---

4. According to the Hindu science called *Nirukta*, resemblances between words are significant and not accidental; the science in question consists in the interpretation of such resemblances.

If this generation could see the hand of God in all things—in the earthquake no less than in the evening calm, in death no less than in life—it would not be what it is; but it only sees blind forces on the one hand and its own temporal desires on the other. This is a delusion. When nothing else is seen, a delusion can become the mainspring of action, and so it is today. Action so motivated is not likely to come to anything, for it is not founded on truth.

God is Truth; the fact that this implies His perfect justice is repugnant to modern sentimental idealism, which, even when it recognizes that on the terrestrial plane there can be no true mercy without justice, still fails to see that God's perfect justice is implicit in His infinite mercy. He will therefore not withhold His hand for ever from those who put idols of their own construction in His place and who attribute their own commonplace ideals to Him.

9

DEVIATION
& PERVERSION

THE distinction between decadence, deviation, and perversion has been set out at the beginning of Chapter 7. The movements, sects, and cults mentioned in Chapter 2, and there referred to as pseudo-religions, are distinguished by the fact that, to whatever extent they can be said to be decadent or deviated, they also embody to a greater or less extent an element of perversion.

Decadence and deviation are ineffectual—they lead anywhere or nowhere; but they serve to open the way to perversion. Perversion is effectual in the sense that it finishes off the work of enfeeblement and loss of direction by distorting the very nature of the things affected by it. The first two could be said to represent passive negation, and the last active negation.

We have seen[1] how negation borrows its nature from that which it denies, having none of its own; it can be regarded as seeking to invert the nature of what it denies. The result of its efforts is therefore always something like an inverted image of what it denies. The more successful it is the more closely the image resembles the model, except in the one particular of being upside down. However, since negation can never be total, on pain of becoming void, the resemblance is never complete. The image is always something of a parody or caricature. It is for reasons of this kind (however they may be expressed) that the pseudo-religions are at one and the same time the things most totally opposed to Religion and its closest imitators.

1. Chap. 3, p 24.

The element of parody is always present, though by no means always equally easy to detect.

The use of the word 'pseudo-religion', which is borrowed from René Guénon, is justified by the fact that the movements, sects and cults in question all profess to provide one or more of the things which it is the exclusive province of Religion to provide. Thus they claim to replace Religion wholly or in part. Whatever may be their claims to the contrary, they are not orthodox in the sense in which the word has been defined earlier, and so are not really Religions. The existence of pseudo-religions only becomes possible when a sufficient number of people have forgotten what Religion is, and the enormous extension of their influence in recent years is but a measure of the increase in that number. The word 'movements' will be used here to denote pseudo-religions collectively, as the least specific word available, despite the fact that any one of their adherents would deny the possibility of dealing with them collectively (if not insofar as movements other than his own are concerned, at least with respect to his own, which, of course, is different).

The number and variety of pseudo-religious movements is great, so that there is a very wide choice, and something to suit the requirements of people of almost every temperament and every taste. Some are well known, highly organized, wealthy and influential in public affairs; others are obscure and difficult to identify, and there is everything in between. There can be little doubt that all their adherents and most of their promoters are sincerely convinced that what they are doing is good. This implies that those adherents are victims of deception; indeed that is the tragedy of the situation. Nevertheless the deceived is not so blameworthy as the deceiver. In any particular case it is always possible that his deception is but temporary or superficial.

Because of its likeness to its model, perversion may be difficult to detect; in this and in all other respects it is satanic in the fullest sense of the word.

Satan aspires first to neutralize the good, and there is no terrestrial good that cannot be neutralized by being separated from its Principle. We have seen this in Chapter 7 in connection with the virtues. Once thus separated, that is to say, not pursued in the name of

God but for its own sake or in the name of anything other than God, the very goodness of the good can be turned into an instrument of deception. For instance, it is sufficiently evident that knowledge, reason, strength and all other powers and faculties can be misapplied and used for evil ends; it is unfortunately less well understood that the greatest evil of all resides in the perversion of things that are assumed to be by nature incorruptible, like beauty, charity, worship and sacrifice, and above all the sacred doctrines, rites and laws. *Corruptio optimi pessima*: the worst of all possibilities is the corruption of the best.

It would not be difficult to list the names of some of the more prominent pseudo-religious movements, but there are reasons against doing so. The most important reason is that any such list would direct attention towards movements that are more or less well established under a distinctive name, and away from those that are less well known or have no distinctive name but are not less important. The latter may prefer to work in secret, or they may have no formal organization, or they may speak in the name of Religion itself.

Those that prefer to work in secret are by definition unknown. Those that have no formal organization can be taken to include all unorganized attempts, literary or otherwise, to meet a 'growing demand for a way of spiritual experience unencumbered by institutional forms'. This quotation is from a notice of a book, and merits a few moments' attention. It would be difficult to devise a neater formulation of the tendency that is at the heart of pseudo-religion. The use of the word 'experience' should be noted in connection with the remarks on pseudo-mystical phenomena that follow; also the implication that the 'institutional forms' of Religion, which must include its rites among other things, are 'encumbrances'. This inference is made plausible by the fact that the forms of Religion can become emptied of their content, as had many of the forms of Judaism at the time of the revelation of Christianity; but it conceals the fact that to seek the content without the form rather than in the form is to court disaster. It is like seeking the way to an unknown place in a trackless desert.

The movements that speak in the name of Religion itself are the most difficult of all to define. Yet if perversion from without is possible, so is perversion from 'within'—and it is bound to occur when traditional authority is weakened and when the forms of Religion are emptied of their content. The matter must be left there, however unsatisfactorily. Nothing less than a special study by a highly qualified person could give a sufficiently well-balanced picture of this extensive realm of border-lines, tendencies and difficult definitions. The decisive role that may be played by an enemy within the gates needs no emphasis. As to the existence of such an enemy and his activity in the world of today, there can be no doubt. There is no copyright in the word 'Christian'; anyone can use it as a label for anything.

Whether they be namable or nameless, all these pseudo-religions are founded upon, or are themselves victims of, the same deception; they therefore have more in common than may appear on the surface, and certainly much more than their mutual contempt and their rivalries would indicate. It may therefore be profitable to consider some of the more important aspects of their deceptiveness, without attempting to attribute any one aspect to any particular movement or movements.

Pseudo-religious movements all justify their existence by offering the fulfillment of a desire that is, at least in some context or other, a desire for the good; and much that they do might, in another context, be productive of good. That desire may be for the acquisition of some power (frequently that of healing), or for some self-improvement in character or in capacity or even in physique, or it may be an ambition to be numbered among an 'elect'. It may also be a simple and sincere desire for a better opportunity to serve God than appears to be available elsewhere. Whatever its precise nature may be, the desire as such often appears to be satisfied, and its satisfaction then convinces the adherent that the method or system or teaching in question works. He is led on by results, whether they be sensory phenomena ('materializations' and the like) or some consciousness of a change for the better in himself or in others, or the acquisition of real or imagined powers, or by an emotional satisfaction proceeding from an act of worship or of charity.

There is no need to question the reality of many of these results; what matters is their significance—or more accurately their lack of significance. Attachment to results is the exact opposite of faith; faith is not faith unless it is unquestioning and unconditional. 'The Lord gave, and the Lord hath taken away; blessed be the name of the Lord,' and 'Though He slay me, yet will I trust in Him,' said Job. God will not be put to the test. 'Thou shalt not tempt the Lord thy God.'

Comparable phenomena can in any case be produced by drugs, by hypnotism, by psycho-analysis and by many other means, diabolical or otherwise. Phenomena as such guarantee nothing and prove nothing. There is no phenomenon, physical or psychic, that cannot be produced in more than one way. In authentic traditional methods and practices their occurrence is regarded with suspicion, and often as one of the main obstacles or temptations with which the devotee has to contend. The results or experiences which these movements provide for their followers may give satisfaction, but it cannot be otherwise than a temporary satisfaction since, despite all claims to the contrary, it is of this world and in no sense spiritual. Insofar as it causes them to accept substitutes for the traditional means of grace, or heresies in place of doctrine (which means untruth in place of truth), it will be not only a false good, but also an active agent of evil.

A large majority of these movements claim an origin in Tradition and an allegiance to Tradition, whether the Tradition in question be living, or long since dead, or even largely imaginary. That claim is only notional, wishful and ineffectual, exactly to the extent that the movement concerned is not orthodox in the sense defined earlier, whatever it may think itself or call itself.

Here again the principle *corruptio optimi pessima* applies, in the sense that the most potentially dangerous movements profess the most exalted spiritual functions or practices or doctrines.

Here we approach an extremely obscure aspect of the question—that concerning the reality or otherwise of an initiation. An initiation is frequently offered by pseudo-religion. Sometimes it may only be a bit of play-acting, in which case it is ineffectual and does not much matter. Sometimes however it may be real, because it goes back in an unbroken line to its origin, and in that case it carries a real spiritual power. Then the question of what use is made of that power becomes one of supreme import, for the very reason that this is the very power which the devil wants most of all to make his own.

When the initiation is accompanied by encouragement to embark on a method of spiritual training, such as is normally reserved for people having special qualifications and working under closely controlled conditions, and when either the qualifications or the conditions are absent, the danger reaches its maximum. The most essential conditions for spiritual training are, first, a full integration of the method and of the individual with the appropriate Tradition and, second, the guidance of a properly qualified master. Neither can be dispensed with.

A mixture of Traditions is characteristic of many pseudo-religious movements. A claim to have picked the best out of the elements of several Traditions is not unknown, incredible though it may seem. It implies a judgment of the greater by the less such as cannot be made with impunity.

It is of course true that adherence to one Tradition does not exclude an understanding of and sympathy for another—very far from it; but that is a very different thing. It is a good deal more than most people can manage to follow one Religion properly, and if its symbolism becomes diluted or obscured, the resultant confusion leaves the individual without a real attachment. It is in this connection that the meeting of East and West has proved most fatal to both.

Many of the movements that have an alien or mixed foundation advise their followers to continue to practice their own Religions, and even to intensify them, often in the name of the universality of their own outlook. They forget that a Religion that needs to be supplemented or diluted from outside is no longer whole. On the contrary, the effectiveness of any single Religion as a means of grace and a way of salvation is impaired or neutralized by its supplementation or dilution with anything that is alien to it. Its wholeness, the harmonious beauty associated with its individuality, is blurred or shattered.

If it is contended that any particular movement is not religious and therefore does not impinge on the field of Religion, it usually shows that the contender does not know what Religion is (and therefore what its field is) nor what allegiance to it implies, particularly in the way of submission to authority. The adoption of a belief or a practice alien to a particular Religion constitutes by itself a denial of the completeness and adequacy of the Religion in question, and implies a half-hearted allegiance to it, one that is lukewarm and is therefore liable to be rejected of God.[2]

There is one other factor that affords something of a key to the parodic character of some of these pseudo-religious movements: it is their fascination with prediction—in which they are by no means alone in the modern world—and in particular with the prediction of a great renewal of Religion, which their followers are allowed or encouraged to assume to be more or less imminent and more or less closely related to their own activities.

Now it is undeniable that the prophetic utterances, scriptural or otherwise, of all Traditions announce the return of a golden age. Prophecy however is far more comprehensive then mere prediction, which is only incidental to its main function, that of a synthetic presentation of truth. The return of a golden age captures the imagination and obscures other predictions no less explicit in prophetic utterances, notably the destruction of the preceding age. However ill acquainted they may be with the Scriptures, almost everyone knows the stories of Noah and of Lot, but almost nobody applies them. Nothing that has been said here must be taken to indicate that a renewal of true Religion is impossible, for it is always possible while the chain of Tradition is intact. But if it came about, the first things to succumb would be the pseudo-religions.

It is, however, not pseudo-religious movements alone, but modernism as a whole, as the embodiment of the profane point of view, which would have to give way to any real renewal of Religion. Pseudo-religion, in all its astonishingly complex and subtle variations and deceptions, can indeed be regarded as the extremity of modernism, a sort of final phase appearing as a reaction against its materialistic aspect. Most of the movements do in fact claim to be

2. Rev. 3:16.

fighting materialism. The crucial question is not how successful or otherwise they may be, but what they are introducing in its stead. To the extent that what they are introducing is but a parody of Religion, all they are doing is to finish off the work already accomplished by materialism.

That work has many aspects. In its earlier stages the main objective is the creation of confusion as to what Religion is and what it is not; this is much the same as to say: between what is good and what is not; or between what is true and what is not. The end of the work is—or would be if it were attainable—a complete inversion of good and evil, truth and untruth. That would be the final triumph of Satan. But, as René Guénon has pointed out, Satan is in reality the most deluded of all beings, because he cannot see that his triumph is at the same time his undoing.

Meanwhile the work of Satan, though it be in principle a work of pure negation, can approach uncomfortably near to completion. A condition of its relative success is obviously the concealment of its nature and intentions. How can it be that they should remain unperceived? It is often said that you cannot fool all the people all the time; it is forgotten that it may be quite sufficient if you can fool enough of the people (and the right ones) for enough of the time. Even the disclosure of a deception that has served its main purpose can play its part, for it concentrates attention on that deception and on the task of its elimination, thereby making the substitution of a new and subtler error much easier.[3]

What of the situation of a person who belongs to one of these pseudo-religious movements, or whose tendencies, in the absence of any formal affiliation, coincide with theirs? The answer can only

3. This is a rule of very wide application in relation to the 'descending' aspect of Tradition; it can be applied to innovations of many kinds, including changes in human institutions, and it is closely related to the understanding of history in its evolutionary aspect. Here however its obvious application is to anti-materialism and to its use as an instrument of deception, despite the fact that in principle it is a sign of discernment and on the side of righteousness. Satanism consists precisely in such conversion to evil ends of things that might be expected to work for good. This position is not affected by the fact that the anti-materialism of many movements is very superficial and has very little relation to their activities.

be that, insofar as any movement or tendency supplants or distorts Religion, it is impossible that it should not be an obstacle to salvation, slight, serious or insuperable as the case may be. But God is the judge, and not we ourselves, so that he would be a rash man who would presume to predict the fate of any individual soul. A right intent may be overlaid by all sorts of apparently unfavorable tendencies; a soul may be immune from perversion in the most adverse circumstances; but such immunity is rare indeed, and the risk is immeasurable, because damage done to the soul is not confined to its life in this world.

Theory, in the sense of something that attaches the mind alone, may not by itself be so dangerous, but the case is different with anything comprising a ritual, or a method of spiritual training, or an initiation, any of which, in relation to the situation of the individual concerned, are unorthodox (even if in another context they might be orthodox), for such things involve the whole being, and not merely a part of it.

It is almost impossible to state a position of this kind fairly without making some kind of reservation that can be seized upon to provide an excuse for rejecting the main statement. Anyone who tries to fathom all the subtleties, tortuosities and plausibilities with which error can clothe itself is doomed to failure. The discernment of spirits is, however, as it were by definition, implicit in the authority of Tradition; when that authority is for any reason inoperative, there can be no sure discrimination, since its judgments alone are based on more than mere opinion.

Is so comprehensive a condemnation of all these pseudo-religious movements and tendencies really justified? Is there nothing good in any of them? They have many millions of followers, most of whom are evidently good, or at least harmless people.

It is true that nothing is wholly bad, but equally true that nothing is wholly good; and here we are concerned not so much with a static quality or condition as with a balance and a tendency. Anything that purports to be spiritual but is not in fact traditional or orthodox, cannot remain merely non-spiritual, but is bound to become anti-spiritual. It cannot remain neutral or harmless for long.

It is also true that the Spirit in its intrinsic reality may obey no rules and conform to no categories: but we are not the Spirit, and unless we obey the rules and conform to the categories so clearly laid down for our good by the Spirit, we are detached from it and lost.

It may be worthwhile to restate very briefly what obedience implies, with reference to the three main elements of Religion. First, a grasp of doctrine, or at least an acceptance of dogma; second, a full participation in the appropriate ritual, not forgetting scriptural reading, canonical prayer and the calendar (that is, feasts of the church, fasts, saints' days, etc.); third, a strict adherence to the appropriate moral code. Added to these, and not less important in its way, is submission to the spiritual authority, which is a practical and effective expression of submission to God; or a symbolical one, which amounts to the same thing.

Once more—without the support, the anchorage, the refuge, the unseen strength and directive force of these things, the soul is almost certain to go astray. The greater its ambitions the more likely it is to do so, and the greater will be its fall if it does. More than ever, in these days of confusion and distraction, it is essential to follow the well-marked path, in the light of the example set by the saints and sages of all time.

11

CORRESPONDENCE WITH THOMAS MERTON

TO LORD NORTHBOURNE, EASTER 1965

I have just finished reading your book *Religion in the Modern World*. Since I did not want to send you a mere formal note of thanks, but wanted also to share my impressions with you, I have delayed writing about it until now.[1]

After a careful reading, spread out over some time (I have read the book a bit at a time), I believe that your book is exceptionally good. Certainly I am most grateful for the opportunity to read it, and needless to say I am very glad that Marco Pallis suggested that you send it to me. Not only is the book interesting, but I have found it quite salutary and helpful in my own case. It has helped me to organize my ideas at a time when we in the Catholic Church, and in the monastic Orders, are being pulled this way and that. Traditions of great importance and vitality are being questioned along with more trivial customs, and I do not think that those who are doing the questioning are always distinguished for their wisdom or even their information. I could not agree more fully with your principles and with your application of them. In particular, I am grateful for

---

1. At the suggestion of Marco Pallis, Lord Northbourne had sent Merton a copy of *Religion in the Modern World*. Merton in turn sent Lord Northbourne a copy of his analysis of Vatican II's Constitution on the Church in the Modern World (*Gaudium et Spes*). Called 'The Church and the "Godless World"', this essay became Part I of Merton's *Redeeming the Time* (published in England by Burns & Oates in 1966). Merton's side of the correspondence reproduced here was first published in *Witness to Freedom: The Letters of Thomas Merton in Times of Crisis*, selected and edited by William H. Shannon (New York: Farrar, Straus & Giroux, 1994).

your last chapter. For one thing it clears up a doubt that had persisted in my mind, about the thinking of the Schuon-Guénon 'school' (if one can use such a term), as well as about the rather slapdash ecumenism that is springing up in some quarters. It is most important first of all to understand deeply and live one's own tradition, not confusing it with what is foreign to it, if one is to seriously appreciate other traditions and distinguish in them what is close to one's own and what is, perhaps, irreconcilable with one's own. The great danger at the moment is a huge muddling and confusing of the spiritual traditions that still survive. As you so well point out, this would be crowning the devil's work.

The great problem that faces me in this regard, is twofold. The Council has determined to confront the modern world and in some way to decide what ought to be its attitude, and where it ought to stand. Now I must say in this area I am very disturbed by both those who are termed conservative and some who are called liberal in the Council, and out of it too. I am afraid that on both sides too superficial a view of 'the world' is being taken—whether that view be optimistic or pessimistic. I don't think that the implications of the technological revolution have even begun to be grasped by either side. Then there is the unfortunate fact that Catholic tradition has become in many ways ambiguous and confused. Not in itself, but in the way in which it is regarded by Catholics. Since people have got into the unfortunate habit of thinking of Tradition as a specialized department of theology, and since spiritual disciplines have undergone considerable shrinking and drying out by being too legalized, and since the traditional styles of life, worship, and so on have become, for us, merely courtly and baroque to such a great extent, the question of renewal does become urgent.

Here is where we run into the greatest difficulties and confusions, especially in America. Personally I can see the wisdom of simply trying to purify and preserve the ancient medieval and earlier traditions which we have in monasticism, and can easily be recovered. Thanks to the work of Solesmes and other monasteries, the material we need is all at hand. Unfortunately it becomes clear that in America at least, and even to some extent in Europe, this will no longer get through to the new generations. And the misfortune is that they seem happy with the most appalling trivialities and the silliest of innovations. In my own work I do my best to keep the novices in touch with monastic sources and convey to them something of the real spirit of monastic discipline and interior prayer. I find that they respond to this, and that the sense of living tradition is not totally dead. But on the other hand, if one is to get into polemics and start battling for tradition, and for right interpretations, one tends oneself to lose the spirit of tradition. And of course perspective and the sense of value disappear along with one's real spirit. If one must choose, I suppose it is best to try oneself to live one's tradition and obey the Holy Spirit within one's tradition as completely as possible, and not worry about results.

More and more I become aware of the gravity of the present situation, not only in matters of tradition and discipline and the spiritual life, but even as regarding man and his civilization. The forces that have been at work to bring us to this critical point have now apparently completely escaped our control (if they were ever under it) and I do not see how we can avoid a very great disaster, by which I do not mean a sudden extermination of the whole race by H-bombs, but nevertheless a general collapse into anarchy and sickness together. In a certain sense, the profound alterations in the world and in man that have resulted from the last hundred years of 'progress' are already a disaster, and the effects will be unavoidable. In such a situation, to speak with bland optimism of the future of man and of the Church blessing a new technological paradise becomes not only absurd but blasphemous. Yet at the same time, this technological society still has to be redeemed and sanctified in some way, not simply cursed and abhorred.

The great problem underlying it also, as you so well see, is idolatry. And here the great question is: can the society we have now constructed possibly be anything else than idolatrous? I suppose one must still hope and believe that it can. But in practice I cannot feel too sanguine about it. In any case, I think we have our hands full seeking and helping the victims of this society, and we cannot yet begin to 'save' and spiritualize the society itself. I am certainly not one of those who, with Teilhard de Chardin, see the whole thing in rosy and messianic colors.

In any case I am very grateful for your important and thoughtful book, and I am sure you can see I am in the deepest possible sympathy with your views. It is not possible for me, and doubtless for you, to get into lengthy correspondence about these things, yet they are so important that I do hope we will be able to share at times ideas and suggestions that might be profitable. I will try to send you some books and writings of my own that you might like. In the book of poems I shall send there is a long letter which you might find interesting, together with a prose poem, 'Hagia Sophia'. I should be most interested in your own writings or statements that might come out from time to time.

LORD NORTHBOURNE'S PRÉCIS OF HIS REPLY

Thanks… welcome exchange of ideas…

Is not the confusion prevalent even in the ecclesiastical hierarchy largely attributable to preoccupation with outward and quantitative results as against inward and qualitative perfection? The Council fails to grasp the implications of technological revolution because pre-occupied with it and not with 'trying to purify and preserve… tradition.'

There could be no worry about the Council's attitude and where it ought to stand if there were no uncertainty about what it, or the Church, really *is*. One fears wrong choice of priorities between outward relations and inward perfection.

A right choice implies that renewal must come about secretly… even 'unintentionally', no particular result being envisaged. If it comes through any organization it will be monastic in spirit even if not in form.

Allusion to Frithjof Schuon's article and forthcoming book. Promise to send.

I question whether 'this technological society still has to be redeemed and sanctified.' God has destroyed societies for their abominations. But never refused Himself to a soul that has remained faithful. Therefore society in His eyes is a framework or testing ground; not it, but souls are precious. It can be sanctified (i.e., when traditional) or not (when otherwise); but souls and not society are saved or dammed. Living now is easy for the body and hard for the soul, in other times it was often the other way round; God will take this into account and not judge us too severely'.

The idea that anything 'positive' can emerge from modern civilization seems heretical, because it postulates that good can come out of evil. Evil posing as good adds to confusion.

Am I muddling redemption, sanctification and salvation and failing to see the sense in which your words are applicable?

Some must battle outwardly, others only inwardly: the latter is the essential—perhaps because it takes no account of results. 'Covet earnestly the best gifts.'

Renewed thanks…

To Lord Northbourne, February 23, 1966

Thank you for your kind letter and for the copy of your lecture, which I read with great interest, finding it clear, objective, and firm. Many thanks also for the first copy of *Tomorrow* in the attractive new format (I very much like the design on the cover). I like this magazine and will be happy to receive it. Last evening I read your article on 'Flowers', which I enjoyed very much. The purely utilitarian explanation of the attractiveness of flowers is always annoying, it is so superficial.

I have written a commentary of the Council's Constitution on the Church in the Modern World. This was done, not because I particularly wanted to do it, but because it was needed as asked for by [the London publisher] Burns and Oates. I am very much afraid that the job is unsatisfactory in many ways. At least I am not at all satisfied with it. The basic purpose of the Constitution is one that I obviously agree with: the maintaining of reasonable communication between the Church and the world of modern technology. If communication breaks down entirely, and there is no hope of exchanging ideas, then the situation becomes impossible. However, the naive optimism with which some of the Council Fathers seem to have wanted a Church entirely identified with the modern scientific

mentality is equally impossible. I have said this in the end as conclu-
sively as I could, with respect to one issue in particular. But in any
case if I can get some copies made of the text I will send you one.
There might be a few points of interest in it. I am of course very
much concerned with one issue which is symptomatic of all the rest:
nuclear warfare. It is true that one should not focus on one issue so
as to distract attention from the entire scene in all its gravity. I think
I have touched on a few other things as well, but have certainly not
done a complete job, and have tried to be conciliatory in some ways.
In a word, I am not satisfied with it and perhaps few others will be.

Meanwhile, as I do have a copy of this meditation on 'events'
['Events and Pseudo-Events', published in *Faith and Violence*, 1968],
I am sending it along. I hope I am not burdening you with too many
things, but obviously I realize that you will not feel obligated to read
them, and will do so only if you are really interested.

To Fr. Thomas Merton August 5, 1966

I have read your commentary on the Vatican Council's Constitution on the Church in the Modern World with great care, and I
hope profitably, and am most grateful to you for sending it. You
provide a very useful explanatory summary and you clarify many
issues. Those issues, I cannot help feeling, important though they
may be, are however subsidiary to something else. I have hesitated
long as to whether I should try to say what it seems to me to be. I do
not see how I can acknowledge your kindness suitably without
attempting to do so. So here goes, as shortly as possible, and therefore perhaps rather violently. What I have to say relates mainly to
the Constitution itself, and only indirectly to your commentary.

We live in a 'Godless' world. What does this mean? It is indisput-
ably a religionless world, unless one stretches the meaning of the
word 'religion' to cover anything one believes to be true, or even
expedient. What I mean is that most people nowadays reject or
ignore the great Revelations and the observances in which they
have been crystallized. They substitute some kind of ideology,
related either to a 'God' of their own invention or to an open

agnosticism. On this view, the world rejects the one true God, and so can properly be said to be Godless, exactly to the extent to which it substitutes a man-made ideology for revealed religion and its crystallizations, or more simply to the extent that it substitutes humanism for religion.

What does the word 'humanism' mean, unless it be the subordination of the essentials of religion to human ideologies? And even if that is not so, I feel sure of one thing, namely, that the distinction between the Christian humanism advocated by the Council and the various other brands of humanism is much too subtle to be grasped by a vast majority of those who take any interest in the matter at all. It is, as you point out, the distinction between treating the individual as 'object' and as 'person', but the metaphysical perception of 'personality' is either absent or is regarded as having been superseded by more recent notions. A scientific and agnostic humanist would argue that exactly what he is out for is the treatment of human beings as 'persons' and not as 'objects', and he will never be able to take the other point of view because it is meaningless to him, as well as to most of his hearers. I wonder if humanism is not always humanism, whatever its label.

What does the Church expect the fate of a Godless world to be? Apparently some kind of humanitarian demi-paradise. Is that what the saints were seeking, or do we know better than they do? The Council may be held to be speaking in the first place to Catholics, who are supposed to know what the true priorities are and to live accordingly—but do they? In any case, is it really prudent (to put it gently) to *appear* not to be putting first things first, despite the danger that religion can always decline into religiosity.

What is a 'better world'? I am perfectly clear as to what it is in the view of a vast majority: it is a more comfortable world, and nothing else. Certainly not a more saintly world—unless humanitarianism is confused with sanctity, as it so often is. A world that is 'better' in any sense of the word, even merely humanitarian, cannot in any case be built out of the material of a Godless world, though it can, and doubtless will, arise out of its ashes. To anyone who can read the signs of the times, the temporal optimism of the Council is hard to justify. I hazard the guess that you have found it so.

There is a statement, quoted by you on page 58, which, if it means what it says, reveals so profound a misconception of the real state of affairs that I can hardly believe my eyes. It says: 'It is now possible to free most of humanity from the misery of ignorance.' The assumption, I suppose, is that modern science has at last revealed the truth and provided the means for its dissemination, or that it has offered hope where before there was none. I am reduced to silence.

I hope you see why such considerations as these seem to me to put all others in the shade, and why I cannot help fearing that this adaption of Christianity to the contemporary mentality has not been carried much farther than is necessary in order to safeguard the very existence of Christianity. As in the past, nothing else can justify a major adaptation, especially coming as it does now with the fullest possible authority of the Church. Or have I completely misinterpreted the tendency of the Constitution?

With one small point in your commentary I cannot agree. You say on page 72 that 'inhumanity is accepted without protest by the vast majority simply because they believe this is the way things have to be.' No, it is because they simply cannot think what to do about it, and no wonder. This feeling of helpless despair counts for much. It is in fact a despair at the failure of humanism, whether they see it as such or not.

One could go on indefinitely. Have I said too much, or just enough, or not enough? The middle course has been my aim.

To Lord Northbourne, August 30, 1966

I am really very grateful for your thoughtful letter [on Merton's 'The Church and the "Godless World"'], and of course you know that I am basically in agreement with you, temperamentally and by taste and background, when it comes to appreciating the values of the ancient cultural and spiritual traditions which today are not only in many ways threatened but even to some extent undermined. And you know, too, that in writing my book on the Constitution on the Church in the [Modern] World, I was not so much trying to clarify a personal philosophy as to interpret what the Council was trying to say, and do so objectively. I have come to the conclusion that the effort was unsatisfactory and have decided not to publish this material in book form in the U.S.A. With this in mind I will take up the points you raise, not with the intention of 'answering' arguments but simply of clarifying my own position—if possible. And it is not easy.

First there was a deliberately permitted ambiguity in the title of the book. There is much discussion now of what it means to be 'godless' and one of the ambiguities about it is that certain Christian values have in fact been smuggled over to the 'godless' side at times. But this too is ambiguous insofar as they tend to become merely 'humanitarian' and so on. But behind the whole question is the fact that the Church has had to admit the futility of an embattled, negative, ghetto-like resistance to everything modern, a 'stance', as they say, which was rather unfortunate in the 19th and early 20th century, not because it was conservative but because it was also quite arbitrary, narrow, uncomprehending, and tended to preserve not necessarily the best of the Catholic tradition but a kind of baroque absolutism in theology, worship, and so on. Now, since the Church obviously has to outgrow this, and since in doing so it has to become for better or for worse 'contemporary', there has been an inevitable reaction, with an insistence on 'openness' and so on which I think is necessary though I do not accept without reservation some of the naive optimism about 'the world' that goes along with this. The general idea is that man has to be understood in his actual present situation, and not with reference to some situation which we would prefer to have him in.

The situation of man today is one of dreadful crisis. We are in full revolution, but it is not the simple, straightforward old-fashioned political revolution. It is a far-reaching, uncontrolled, largely unconscious revolution pervading every sphere of his existence and often developing new critical tendencies before anyone realizes what is happening. Now, I think that the Constitution, though it does vaguely recognize this, does not say enough to underline the real seriousness of the situation, and it does, as you say, tend to accept the surface optimism of some secular outlooks on progress without much hesitation. It does seem to say that if we just go along with technology we will have a happier and better world. This is by no means guaranteed. On the other hand, I do not feel, as some do, that the Constitution should simply have admitted frankly that the future promises little more than apocalyptic horror. Though this possibility is very real and was perhaps not brought out very clearly. In other words I think the attitude taken by the Council is basically reasonable, and it seems to be this:

Much as we appreciate the great value of ancient and traditional cultures, the coming of the industrial and technological revolution has undermined them and in fact doomed them. Everywhere in the world these cultures have now been more or less affected—corrupted—by modern Western man and his rather unfortunate systems. It is simply not possible to return to the cultural stability and harmony of these ancient structures. But it is hoped that one can maintain some sort of continuity and preserve at least some of their living reality in a new kind of society. For my part I am frankly dubious: I foresee a rather pitiful bastardized culture, vulgarized, uniform, and full of elements of parody and caricature, and perhaps frightening new developments of its own which may be in a certain way 'interesting' and even exciting. And terrible. The Council assumes that we just go on peacefully progressing and reasonably negotiating obstacles, making life more and more 'human'.

I certainly think that we need a much 'better' world than the one we have at the moment, and I make no bones about insisting that this means feeding, clothing, housing, and educating a lot of people who are living the most dreadful destitution. Remember that in South America, Africa, Asia, we are no longer comparing the ancient tribal cultures with modern culture but the rural and urban slum culture of destitution and degradation that has ruined and succeeded the old cultures. This *must* be dealt with, and in facing the fact the Church has simply done her plain duty: and a great deal more needs to be done on the spot. It is a well-known fact that if in South America the people who call themselves Catholics would get down to work and do something about the situation, it could be immensely improved. Hence I see nothing wrong with the Council demanding work for a 'better world' in this sense. It is not a question of comfort, but of the basic necessities of life and decency. In this respect, 'humanism' is a matter of simple respect for man as man, and Christian humanism is based on the belief in the Incarnation and on a relationship to others which supposed that 'whatsoever you do to the least of my brethren you do it to me' (i.e., to Christ). Here I have no difficulty. Except of course in the way in which some of this might be interpreted or applied. Literacy is not a cure-all, and there are plenty of absurd modern social myths. Nevertheless there are realities that must be faced in the terms of our actual possibilities, and return to the ancient cultures is simply not possible. Though we should certainly try to see that their values are preserved insofar as they can be.

Since the purpose of this Constitution was that of giving largely practical directives for the way in which Catholics should participate in the work of trying to help man through his present crisis, the 'first things' were simply stated in a few obvious broad principles in the place where this was most relevant: beginning of the Constitution, beginning of various sections, and so on. It must be remembered that the Constitution is part of a whole, and the work of the Council fills a volume of nearly eight hundred pages in the edition I have. The 'first things' are treated much more extensively in places like the Constitution on the Church and on Revelation. But in practice, with man in a position literally to destroy himself and his culture, I do not think that concern about saving him temporally and giving him a chance to set his house in order is merely secondary.

It is for this reason that I cannot take a merely conservative position, though I see a great deal wrong and suspect about the progressive view and I do not find myself always able to speak its language. But I wonder if the traditional spiritual language of charity and mercy does not in fact demand to be put into action in these social forms in our new situation. But of course here we are in a realm where I cannot competently speak. I am not an economist or a politician.

In any case I really appreciate your letter. Doubtless it was my own fault if the book was not clear and gave the impression that this was just a matter of the 'social gospel' over again. It is much more a problem than that.

Stated in the baldest terms, in my own situation, I meet the problem daily in this form: I can completely turn my back on the whole 'world' and simply try to devote myself to meditation and contemplation, silence, withdrawal, renunciation, and so on. I spent at least twelve years of my monastic life with no further object than this. At the end of that time I began to see that this was insufficient and indeed deceptive. It was unreal. It could indeed create in me the impression that I was putting first things first and striving for sanctity. But I also learned in many ways that it was false and that the whole thing rested on a rather imaginary basis. I still devote most of my time to meditation, contemplation, reading—in fact I now give much more of my time to these things since I am living in solitude: but also I read a great deal more about what is happening and the common problems of the world I live in, not so much on the level of newspapers (I do not get the paper) or of magazines, still less radio or TV (I have barely seen TV once or twice in my life). But I do feel that if I am not in some way able to identify myself with my contemporaries and if I isolate myself so entirely from them that I imagine that I am a different kind of being, I am simply perpetrating a kind of religious fraud. I quite simply believe that I have to hear the voice of God not only in the Bible and other writings, but in the crisis of this age, and I have to commit myself to a certain level of responsibility: in my case being a writer I have to be able to speak out and say certain things that may need saying, to the best of my knowledge and according to my conscience and to what seems to be the inspiration of the Holy Spirit. I realize the enormous difficulty of this, and I have no illusion that it is easy to be a prophet, or that I must necessarily try to be one. But there are things I think I must say. In the case of the book about the Council Constitution, however, I am, I think, quite aware that what I was saying did not need to be said, at least by me, and I have decided that there is no point in having the book published here. It is not the kind of thing I am supposed to be doing.

In the long run, I think that is what you were trying to tell me in your letter, and I quite agree.

Thus you see that in the end we do meet, though I think there are genuine accidental differences in our viewpoint. I think you are simply more straightforwardly conservative than I am and that for you the conservative position does not present the difficulties that it does for me. You are fortunate, because your position is thus much simpler than mine can be, and it is easier for you to be quite definite on every point where I might have to hesitate and qualify. In fact there are many points that are to me uncertain, and I cannot say what I think about them.

To Fr. Thomas Merton, October 9, 1966

Thank you very much for your letter of 30th August. It has been helpful to me in clearing my own head, and in giving me a broader view of the nature and intentions of the Constitution on the Church in the Modern World. In one respect my position is indeed 'simple' and as 'conservative' as you like—but only in one. If I have given the impression of being definite on every point (your penultimate remark) it is my fault, for that is the last thing I would profess to be. It is not the same thing as being definite on *one* point, as I am (if it can be called a single point), and then trying to relate other points to it. That is where complexity and uncertainty come in, for me as for you, and they tend all too often to obscure the main issue. So may I try to clarify?

In the present context, my one point could be expressed, among endless other possible ways, as follows. You cannot give yourself to mankind in charity unless you have first given yourself to God. If you try to do so your gift will be valueless—it will be giving a stone for bread—or worse, giving for a fish a serpent. (There is a more positive corollary to this: if you give yourself to God, you are thereby giving yourself to mankind.) Surely this is the essence of the teaching of the Gospels (summarized in the two commandments), the first element in Christian charity, and so in man's duty to man. If that is not so, I am beating the air. But because I believe it to be so, I cannot but feel that the Council could have insisted on this essential point, again and again and again, without being any less specific about the application of this principle to the particular problem in view. Some such insistence would seem to be specially important in this particular section of the whole work of the Council, simply because the principle in question is the very one that scientific humanism seeks above all to eliminate, knowing that victory depends on its elimination; scientific humanism parodies Christian charity by substituting terrestrial welfare for salvation. Hitherto the Roman Catholic Church has been the arch-opponent of this heresy. She has not only put first things first, but has also appeared to do so. If she ceases to maintain an uncompromising position in this one respect, what may not the end be? *Quis custodiet ipsos custodes?*

The Constitution on the Church in the Modern World, besides receiving much more publicity than any other part of the Council's work, has been widely accepted as a pronouncement which stands on its own. There is no indication to the contrary in the English translation published by Burns & Oates for the Catholic Truth Society (which is the one I have).

That seems to me to be the starting-point, which admits of no compromise, to which all else must be made to conform, whatever the immediate cost of conformity may appear to be. That is my case. I do not suppose for a moment that yours is any different. If we differ it is only in details of its application to this or that problem.

I was much interested in what you say about your own situation. I suppose that the art of living could be said to consist largely in recognizing one's own vocation, and acting accordingly. I feel sure that my vocation is not that of a monk or hermit. (If it is, I have missed it!) I did not begin to see things consciously as I do now till nearly 50 (I am now 70). By that time my 5 children had already arrived (and have since proliferated into an additional 12) and I was thoroughly involved in the affairs of a hereditary landowner and farmer. Such has been my destiny and I should be the last to quarrel with it. One must do what one can within the framework of one's destiny. Are you not by vocation a preacher? Preaching covers writing, especially in these days. If so, you seem to have followed it to some effect. Others are pure contemplatives, and I would on no account depreciate the importance of the part they are called upon to play. In these days destiny is disregarded and vocation is suppressed. We imagine that we control not only our own future, but also our own nature. No delusion could be more unfortunate. We are terribly like the Laodiceans in Revelations, chap. 3, especially verse 17.[2] It is easy enough at the moment to see the temporal and tenebrous aspect of existence; less easy to see its eternal and luminous aspect. Yet the latter is the reality.

P. S. I see in today's *Times* that Dr Eric Fromm, 'analyst and thinker,' self-described as a 'Neo-Freudian more Freudian that the Freudians,' says he 'sees today a whole movement of humanism in which Roman Catholics, Protestants, and Marxists have more in common than separates them.' This has special relevance to the middle of page 86 above. I suggest that what they have in common is precisely their animality.

To Lord Northbourne, June 4, 1967

To begin with, I am more and more convinced that *Redeeming the Time* is a superficial and inadequate book. I do, of course, believe still in the urgency of social change in places like South America, where, frankly, too many people are living in appalling conditions, brought on in many cases by 'progress'. In any event, this book is not being published anywhere else.

What really prompted me to write to you today: I am reading a curious book called *Evolution and Christian Hope* by one Ernst Benz. Curious is not the word for parts of it. He has a chapter which justifies technological progress by the Bible and by ideas like God the potter framing his creatures on a potter's wheel. And he finds in Catholic medieval tradition (where the Victorines for instance speak of the 'arts' in terms like Marco Pallis) warrant for the idea that 'technology is a means of overcoming original sin.' I thought that gem of modern thought should be shared with you. Fantastic, isn't it? Really, you are so very right. That is what we are facing now. I do not suggest that you read this book, it would shock you. But that particular chapter is so funny, in its own bizarre way, that you might dip into it there if the book ever comes your way.

---

2. 'For you say, I am rich, I have prospered, and I need nothing; not knowing that you are wretched, pitiable, poor, blind, and naked.'

But I do not suppose it will, and do not encourage you to go looking for it.

I just thought I would send you these few badly typed lines as a sign of life and a reminder that I do very much appreciate all that you have to say, and that I am very aware of the ambiguities of the current Catholic position. I am frankly quite alienated from much of the thinking going on in my Church, on both sides, both conservative and 'progressive'.

INDEX

Printed in the United Kingdom
by Lightning Source UK Ltd.
126924UK00001B/211/A